The Daughter's Exchange

The African American Woman's Encounter with the Intellectual Marketplace

a vernacular performance

V Efua Prince

To Bell

Alternative Book Press
2 Timber Lane
Suite 301
Marlboro, NJ 07746

www.alternativebookpress.com

Daughter's Exchange

2018 Paperback Edition
Copyright 2018 © V Efua Prince
Cover Design by CL Smith

Cover Illustration by Steve Prince
Book Design by Alternative Book Press
All rights reserved
Published in the United States of America by Alternative Book Press. Originally published in electronic form in the United States by Alternative Book Press.

Publication Data
V. Efua Prince [2018]
Daughter's Exchange/ by V. Efua Prince—1sted.

Ask Publisher for Further Publication Information

ISBN 978-1-940122-41-0 Printed in the United States of America 10 9 8 7 6 5 4 3 2 1

The Daughter's Exchange

The African American Woman's Encounter with the Intellectual Marketplace

a vernacular performance

V Efua Prince

TABLE OF CONTENTS

ACKNOWLEDGMENTS	iv
INTRODUCTION	1
Chapter 1 INTERCOURSE	22
Inheritance	36
Omo-osu	82
Baba	112
Chapter 2 POWER	152
Abidemi	167
Palava	198
Ex-*Ile*	228

Chapter 3	HAMBONE	263
Resistance		274
Amita		284
Marketplace		329

ACKNOWLEDGMENTS

Thank you

Monifa Love Asante
Lois Benjamin
Caroline Brown
Amee Carmines
Rebecca Dixon
Lloren Foster
Yao Glover
William R. Harvey
Cynthia Holier-Fatton
Deborah McDowell
Renee Moreno
Marlon Ross
Rion Amilcar Scott
Ian G. Strachan
Thabiti Willis

With love and sincere gratitude

Imani
Elijah
Etienne
Bobby
& Lurlene

And to you

Father
for your gracious inspiration.

INTRODUCTION

> If *oriki* remove categorical barriers that hinder the flow of power from one being to another, it is their apparent formlessness that enables them to do so.
>
> —Karin Barber, *I Could Speak Until Tomorrow*

ònà ló jin, erú náà ní baba
he may be far away but the slave has a father too[1]

In *Modernism and the Harlem Renaissance* Houston Baker recasts the perception asserted by scholars like Nathan Huggins and David Levering Lewis who saw the Harlem Renaissance as a "failure"—having been unsuccessful in transforming the social order for African Americans—by reading the distinct characteristics of black modernist production as a "family affair." In the framework Baker lays out in *Modernism*, he deliberately argues that academic and cultural production emerge out of the intimate bonds of family and a personal history leading back to the economics of slavery. By explicitly drawing on family ties, Baker hopes to situate African American cultural productions of the early twentieth century within a frame of reference that validates the lived experiences of black people, whose identities like that of Booker T. Washington, were forged and cultivated within the postbellum conditions of the Jim Crow South.

Baker's reflections on his father create a point of entrée for himself, and African Americans more generally, into the academic discussion of modernism; furthermore, he suggests that the "children" of his father's generation—a generation that became the architects of the blues—have inherited a sense of responsibility as well as blues sensibilities. The Harlem Renaissance was successful, in Baker's estimation, because it fostered a spirit of nationalism in successive generations. He argues that judgments about the impact Alain Locke, Langston Hughes, Countee Cullen, Jessie Fauset, Dorothy West, Wallace Thurman, and others had upon the nation have been skewed by scholars's reluctance to read their work and contributions through the valiance of African American culture. Baker writes:

> I came to realize that much of what passes for self-consciously "scholarly" effort on the part of black men and women in the United States is often production self-consciously oriented to win approval from those who have a monopoly on definitions of SCHOLARSHIP. "Careerism" is one sign for the black scholar's inclination to preserve the critical vocabulary *and* the

> assumptions of a dominating culture in his or her analyses of his or her own "dominated" culture. Another term is "conservatism," and still another, I believe, is "fear." All three produce the same result—the enhancement of the dominating society's power (xvii).

By the time Baker makes this observation he has, of course, won "approval from those who have a monopoly on definitions of SCHOLARSHIP," becoming a full professor at an ivy league (which is to say "exclusive") institution, as a result of his own "self-consciously 'scholarly' effort"—his prose in his most widely read work, *Blues, Ideology and Afro-American Literature: A Vernacular Theory*, is nearly impossible to read at times. Thus, the extent to which Baker has been successful in utilizing a black scholarly apparatus might well be debated.

Nevertheless, Baker's observation is still apropos, and the question at work here is similar to the one Eric Sundquist suggests under girds the *Plessy v Ferguson* decision: "Who can *appear* to be white?" The question implied by Baker and more directly relevant to the issues explored in each of these chapters is: Who can *appear* to be a scholar? Certainly individuals like Baker and another leading African Americanist, Henry Louis Gates, Jr., *appear scholarly* even while they bring African American culture in the form of the vernacular into the academic marketplace by drawing on the ideology of the blues and the African linguistic traditions respectively; but their reliance on highly specialized academic discourse reifies the primacy of the linguistic sign over the other kinds of cultural production they claim to champion. In other words, their published work primarily addresses concerns utilizing language that has been the domain of white, male academics rather than that of the black folk, which is the source of their vernacular culture. Gates's signifyin(g) monkey, for example, is an overt attempt to locate African and African American word play within semiotics. Even Baker, whose reading of the blues arises out of a Marxist philosophy that emphasizes material production, turns his attention to the metatext of physics and extraterrestrial "black (w)holes"—a move that expands the boundaries of African American cultural production even as it removes the work from its cultural foundation. It might be true that the resulting distance between these modes of production does not necessarily suggest a break even if it suggests a departure, which some may argue is a necessary by product of the academic process. But my work explores another possibility.

We find a ready framework for building on Gates's use of the Middle Passage and its resulting impact and on Baker's deliberate articulation of the blues as ideology in the *oriki* performed by women in Yoruba West Africa. As anthropologist Karin Barber explains, "The word *oriki* is used in Yoruba academic writing to translate the English word 'definition,' for *oriki* are felt to encapsulate the essential qualities of entities" (12). In another place, Barber adds that fundamentally, the *oriki* performance is an act of naming (67). But the *oriki* are not academic texts. They are chants, which are difficult to codify as literary genres. Generally, literary theorists have dismissed the textual merit of *oriki* because its form is so foreign when compared to European literature. Unlike the Aristotelian notion of structure, *oriki* has no beginning, middle, or end; nor does one necessarily follow another in any given order. *Oriki* cannot be attributed to any particular author. And they are common, being performed by women during any number of ceremonial and everyday tasks. "The women [who perform *oriki*] do not call it by any name or classify the great variety of their production according to style, subject matter or musical mode. It is difficult to detach, as an object of study, from the context of its performance..." (Barber 12). By insisting, through the very mode of production, that its performance remain grounded in the social interplay of the work-a-day world rather than in academic halls where things are codified and compartmentalized, *oriki* offer us a means of engaging not just the vernacular but also the mundane.

    The mundane is vital to our lives; nevertheless these everyday activities are so common and so terrestrial that we treat them, well, like dirt. However, Barber identifies *oriki* as a "master discourse" (1) in an effort to legitimize her attempt to bring the form into the intercourse. Intercourse, the free exchange of ideas across broadly defined groups, is at the heart of the academic process. Discourse, which is a more narrow conversation occurring within the academic community, masks itself as intercourse in order to conceal its exclusivity. Ostensibly, graduate school teaches us how to participate in academic discourse but engaging the broader intercourse is an entirely different task.

According to womanist scholar Karla Holloway, the move from discourse to intercourse occurs when literary theorists engage in the process of naming. "It seems to me," she writes, "that when the process of naming is an activity of a community formed as a result of a dialogic relationship between the world and the word, then the nature of that naming process has shifted from a naming of the discourse of criticism to naming *as discourse in* criticism. Such a shift neither privileges the community nor its activity, but creates instead a dynamic and creative intercourse between the two, a call and response..." (53). This is an apt description for the performance of *oriki,* which as Barber suggests, represents a heightened form of dialogue (249). Holloway's emphasis is on the dialogue occurring within a community that identifies interpretive parameters without limiting discursive terrain. In these terms, *oriki* works like literary theory to name and to define the "dimensions of the interpretive community" (53) through the process of creative interplay. This interplay happens between past and present agents, living and dead, spirit and flesh, us and them, here and there (geographically and otherwise), across genders and generations.

Nevertheless it is difficult for black women who participate in these mundane exchanges to join the intercourse outside of their immediate communities. In order to meaningfully engage similarly dialogical processes that function *as discourse in* criticism, black women must be allowed to utilize a language that best expresses their experiences; my emphasis being not on the words themselves but on the substance they evoke. *Oriki* does this by having a speaking subject present in the performance, while subverting the notion of "authority" through the inclusion of traditional verses that represent the absent presence of other speaking subjects. The ancestral voices retained in the performance recall rather than repress their invisible (absent) presence alongside the current speaker. In this context, the word is not predominant; instead the performer's ability to define the present experience in continuity with the past and foreseeable future is more significant. Such a process signals a shift from the signifier to the signified, from an emphasis on the language to that of lived experience. Very often the experiences that make up our daily lives carry little intrigue for anyone except those who are directly involved with them but for direct participants in these mundane activities, the daily drama may be all consuming.

Traditional academic discourse favors the semblance of objective, universal truth by masking the agent behind the language, but I resist this move by drawing upon *oriki* as an African and woman centered oral practice. While the former emphasizes the signifier—meaning the authority of the word—the latter emphasizes the signified—meaning the experience represented through the act of naming or the vernacular performance. Although all of this occurs in language, one tradition has sought to erase the body of lived experience while the other seeks to reify it. Of course, I cannot escape the system of language which I am critiquing because in making my argument I am clearly signifying in the traditions of both Saussure and the signifyin' monkey of black vernacular. However, my hope is to continually remind the reader of the agents behind the text rather than to obscure those collectively engaged in defining the "dimensions of [my] interpretive community." As another point of note, I make generalizations throughout the text about the nature of western discourse and about the nature of *oriki*. In so doing, I mean to evoke the rule rather than the exception, of which there are naturally too many to name. My goals are literary rather than historical or anthropological. Neither do I intend to suggest that any of the discursive practices engaged here is either intrinsically liberating or essentially oppressive. My premise is that they are mythical and utilized to meet the aims of those who wield them.

In Yoruba West Africa, women find relative expressive freedom in the private, public space of their *ile*. On these homegrounds, where people recognize bonds of kinship, women are able to call for help from the living and the dead, draw power from their God, give voice to fear, offer praise to great men, memorialize the past, name the present, predict the future, and readily add their voices to a dynamic art. However, as Adélékè Adéékó notes, traditionally *oriki* have served the power in place[2]. Voices of the subaltern, Adéékó maintains, are left silent in the gaps and disjunctures inherent in the form (190). *Oriki* quiet dissent and subdue the voices of those who might otherwise recall unconscionable acts like trading slaves across the Atlantic, for instance. The liberatory nature of word play has its limits. That is why I privilege the signified over the signifier, experience over the word, *ile* over *oriki*. My ancestors were among those ruthlessly silenced within those gaps. My genealogy is not recorded in song; instead, it was deliberately erased and my heritage alternately stolen and discarded. This systematic attempt to destroy all ties with the past, distinguishes the history of African Americans from other populations and we have been left without an *oriki orile*, a family narrative to be passed through generations. Nevertheless, we have lived.

The incontrovertible evidence of African American history is recorded in our lives, consequently the lived experiences of African American women is inherently valuable. Of course, the marketplace does not agree. The final section of this study is dedicated to a discussion of the marketplace. In Nigeria, even after colonization, the market remains woman centered and can be liberating for women. Unfortunately, the African market is circumscribed for me by the slave market and the more immediate pressures of the academic market. In this context, the Nigerian market, too, has limitations. In Yoruba Nigeria *itan*, the formal history that presents the public face of the society, is traditionally the province of respected, older men—paralleling academic practices, including those at the foundation of African American studies. *Oriki* is given to the women as a means of supporting the given order: young girls serve as chorus while attending a bride; young women perform publicly just before marrying often older men who may already have other wives; and skilled women praise "Big Men" on their heritage and their admirable qualities. These public performances support the private affairs of men.

This dichotomy of men and women might impose a reductive Western notion upon a culture with a more sophisticated conception of gender due, at least in part, to the more complex family structures created by polygamy. Oyèrónké Oyéwúmí notes that the ìdílé (lineage) represented by the *oriki orile* are not simple patrilineages as presumed by Western scholars since, "Mothers and female offspring are as central in the determination of the identity and characteristics of these institutions as are fathers and male offspring. The patrilineage is not so much the father's house as the father's house as inflected by the mother's identity" (106). Moreover, personal *oriki* are performed sometimes for exceptional women noting their accomplishments, particularly at funerals, and some *oriki* challenge the existing order by pitting one family against another perhaps more politically powerful family. However, the resistance they offer to the existing power structure is nominal.

I do not wish to nor am I able to adopt this cultural practice wholesale. My effort is to subvert the established order that exiled my ancestors and subjected them to the horrors of the transatlantic slave trade. And to speak from the chasm in patriarchal discourse, be it Eurocentric or Afrocentric, into which the African American woman's experience has been discarded. I am defining the dimensions of a homeground of sorts that affords me access, if not to the broader marketplace, then to a more private audience where bonds of kinship permit me to speak.

My intent is to give new definition to Suzan-Lori Parks and Zora Neale Hurston by situating them within a fluid textual performance. This study borrows some formal elements from *oriki* in that it seeks to name Parks and Hurston as "Big Women" writers[3] and to identify their patrilineal intellectual heritage (*orile*) and to ground my reading of them within a broad geography (*ile*) of African American voices. The thrust of this work moves us from language (*oriki*), which is circumscribed by male sites of power, to home (*ile*), specifically Georgia which is the site of my own familial homeground. I draw upon multiple voices, those of the fathers (*baba*) like Plato, Shakespeare, Locke, Chesnutt, Derrida, John Edgar Wideman, Houston Baker, and his protégé, Michael Awkward, and familiar voices of the daughters (*omo-osu*) like Suzan-Lori Parks, Zora Neale Hurston, Alice Walker, and those of unknown daughters (still *omo-osu*) like my student Violet and my great aunt Clydie. Like all attempts to locate and categorize human experience, this effort involves a good measure of mythology such as the story of Jezebel and a Yoruba creation story and perhaps even a little back talk of my own.

This text functions like *oriki*, which "are not 'history' in the sense of an overview or attempt to make sense of a sequence of events, but a way of experiencing the past by bringing it back to life" (Barber 15), this work recalls bits of a fragmented, sometimes academic, sometimes distant and sometimes very personal past. These fragments are brought together to create the sense of a whole rather than a conventional Aristotelian structure. And because I move with little regard for beginnings or endings the composite gains significance. Biographical detail about Zora Neale Hurston's life is interwoven with narrative, for instance, infusing both with new meaning. So although the order in which information is presented is less important in this context, the experience of the *whole* vernacular performance becomes rather important.

In other words, a reader cannot necessarily anticipate the content of one section by looking at another as we might in more conventional studies (i.e. the ending does not necessarily suggest what came before it nor does the first or second section necessarily anticipate the subsequent sections). Shifts are sometimes signaled by formal section breaks with chapter headings or subheadings. Frequently, shifts to a personal narrative are marked by a typographical change to italics or a section might break and begin again with another thought. These stylistic shifts are deliberate attempts to utilize a vernacular structure to "speak from the gaps" inherent in conventional texts. If a black woman is denied the privilege of utilizing her personal experiences as the rich cultural base of her intellectual work then she is robbed of the wealth of her inheritance. To reflect on these experiences is to seek ties to an ancestral past that may ground her in the way that Toni Morrison suggests as "rootedness." And in looking back, she is necessarily seeking to uncover some truth about herself.

What follows in the first chapter is a broad exploration of terms introduced in Plato's *Symposium* as well as Shakespeare and the Bible that will be reiterated throughout the study. Sycorax, Caliban's mother in *The Tempest*, helps situate the dilemma African American women confront upon entering Western discourse. However, Sycorax along with Suzan-Lori Park's Hesters and Hottentot Venus are fertile, black women who are disenfranchised even as their progeny (both real and imagined) linger as monstrous reminders of the complexities involved in moral claims for restitution.

In the second chapter, I set Zora Neale Hurston's biography against a narrative that has been fictionalized to protect the identities of those involved in the actual incidents and read them through a valence of Yoruba mythology. I introduce the story of Esu's birth as a means of expanding the discursive grounds of Hurston's now familiar story to situate her as an ex-*ile* (pairing the Latin and the Yoruba). Such a move allows me to demonstrate the ways that many of the struggles Hurston confronted in her life continue to resonate in the contemporary narrative about African American women scholars who sometimes must still face coercive abuse of power.

Finally in the third chapter, Charles Chesnutt's *The Marrow of Tradition* lays the foundation for the literary tradition emerging at the dawn of the twentieth century, but the heart of my argument is comprised of the story of my great aunt Clydie. In recuperating Clydie's story, I examine various aspects of her lived experience—her spent life. The spent life is a bounded progression of time that has been exchanged for a particular set of human experiences. In circulating Clydie's story within the academic marketplace, I examine the ways that women have learned to account for the "spent" life of their predecessors. *The Daughter's Exchange* is an exploration of the very marrow of our traditions that takes us around the world (ex*ile*) but also brings us back again (*ile*).

Works Cited

Adeeko, Adeleke. "Oral Poetry and Hegemony: Yoruba Oriki." *Dialectical Anthropology.* 26(2001): 181-192. University of Virginia. Springer Link. 23 October 2008.

Baker, Houston A., Jr. *Modernism and the Harlem Renaissance.* Chicago: University of Chicago Press, 1987.

Barber, Karen. *I Could Speak Until Tomorrow: Oriki, Women and the Past in a Yoruba Town.* Edinburgh University Press for International African Institute, 1991.

Holloway, Karla. *Moorings and Metaphors: Figures of Culture and Gender in Black*

Women's Literature. New Brunswick, NJ: Rutgers University Press, 1992.

Oyèrónké Oyéwúmí. *The Invention of Women: Making an African Sense of Western Gender Discourse.* Minneapolis: University of Minnesota Press, 1997.

CHAPTER 1

INTERCOURSE

> CALIBAN: You taught me language, and
> my profit on't
> Is, I know how to curse.
> —Shakespeare, *The Tempest*

baba mi ó ní ohun eni ní í moni lára
my father, he said, 'Having one's own things is
really more convenient'[4]

Notwithstanding the prominence to which some African American women writers have risen in the latter half of the twentieth century, more often than not, the place assigned to the black woman in the history of western letters is tangential to the action of the story and she remains largely absent from direct participation in the surrounding intercourse. Consequently, when she is represented it is as others see her, often projecting their anxieties, desires, and fears onto her. The African American woman confronts these representations as narrowly defined stereotypes, which are necessarily painful and reductive. If she is able to do something that effects a change in her life or the lives of others without willing self-sacrifice then she is decidedly anti-social, if not evil and dangerous. If she is attractive, she is a whore. If she is strong, she turns men to stone. If she possesses knowledge that others do not understand then she is a witch, like Sycorax. Sycorax is a woman from northern Africa who was banished for her misdeeds to an island in Shakespeare's *The Tempest* where she raises her son Caliban in relative isolation. She lords over the island until her death leaves her son ill equipped to defend the oasis from intruders. Caliban loses authority of the island after teaching Prospero the secrets of Sycorax's conjure. Prospero, the ousted Duke of Milan, along with his daughter Miranda, displaces

Sycorax and her son as ruler of the mystical island. Having acquired power over the environment, Prospero usurps Caliban's position as the natural king. On the other hand, Caliban has learned enough of Prospero's books from Miranda for him to hate them, as they represent Prospero's authority.

Caliban subverts Miranda's efforts to endow his "purposes With words that made them known" (I ii 359-60) by learning to curse. While much discussion has occurred on the subject of Caliban's curses, my attention is drawn to his mother. The overwhelming volume of scholarly interest in Caliban's declaration that "You taught me language, and my profit on't Is, I know how to curse" (I ii 365-366) reflects the academic predisposition to emphasize the language, the signifier, meanwhile the signified, the substance and meaning of Sycorax's life, for example, is hidden behind Caliban's curses. Sycorax is the foreign presence whose dark influence becomes menacing not because of what she speaks (in fact we never hear from her) but because she gives birth to and nourishes the more threatening figure of Caliban. Beyond his mother, Caliban's ancestry is unclear since his paternity is never mentioned. In effect, Caliban is raised by a single-parent, so when he "goes bad," we have only his mother—and the apparent dysfunction inherent in matriarchy—to blame.

Perhaps it is the dysfunction of this family that draws Houston Baker's attention to *The Tempest* in his study on black modernism. While, as I have mentioned, Baker emphasizes his own paternity as a means of justifying his critical engagement (which might explain his focus on the impact of Prospero's "mastery" on Caliban), his familiarity with the rhetoric of family dysfunction, that tends to "blame the mother" and lament the "absent father," helps him offer a more sympathetic reading of Sycorax's position: "The Western Renaissance 'storm' displaces in fact the witch as worker of sounding magic and releases, in her place, the comprador spirit Ariel who aids Prospero's male manipulations" (Baker 55). Prospero seemingly manages to transcend the bodily limitations that constrain Sycorax, who not only bears a grotesque son but ultimately succumbs to her mortality.

The dichotomy we see established in *The Tempest* between the terrestrial African mother and the numinous Western father is manifested repeatedly throughout literature. As that African mother Sycorax is displaced by the "Western Renaissance 'storm'," in part, because she is not there to begin with. The "rebirth" fostered by this period of growth in Western culture is conceived in the white, male mind rather than in the black, female body. Thus in *The Tempest* the actual woman is removed and the island becomes a surrogate for Sycorax's body; her lingering earthly mysteries are now administered humanely by Prospero's fatherly hand but Caliban remains as a sign of her monstrous potential to be unruly and let loose. Sycorax is the learned, powerful, dark woman whose accursed seed threatens to deflower and defile future generations. Prospero imprisons Caliban, we gather, to restrict his access to Miranda. Prospero's fears are voiced by Caliban who laments, "O ho, O ho! Would't had been done! Thou didst prevent me; I had peopled else This isle with Calibans" (I ii 351-53). By the end of the play Prospero's line promises to remain pure through Miranda's marriage to

Ferdinand while Sycorax's line will end with her illegitimate heir frustrated by the curse of servitude.

Because *The Tempest* reflects the growing anxiety over an expanding world view during a time of geographical exploration and cultural confrontation, African Americans like Baker and John Edgar Wideman read the play as an apt metaphor for key aspects of black experiences in America. *The Tempest* and Caliban's thwarted relationship with Miranda is central to John Edgar Wideman's novel *Philadelphia Fire*. The protagonist, Cudjoe is a writer who has returned to Philadelphia from his self-imposed exile on a Greek island after the 1985 bombing of an organization called MOVE that burned down an entire city-block. Before leaving Philadelphia to spend ten years acting out the role of Caliban on an island in the Mediterranean, the author prepared a class of students at the school where he taught to perform the play. Unfortunately, the performance is doused by two days of stormy weather, a fitting end to an improbable scene—a group of black urban youth reciting Shakespeare in the park.

For a while, however, the writer imagines his students as Caliban with a decidedly urban twist. Rather than lie prone and passively receive Miranda's lessons Wideman writes:

> Caliban, witches' whelp that he was, had a better idea. Her need, his seed joined. An island full of Calibans. He didn't wish to be run through her copy machine. Her print of goodness stamping out his shape, his gabble translated out of existence. No thanks, ma'am. But I will try some dat poontang. Some that ooh la la, oui, oui goodness next to your pee-pee. Which suggestion she couldn't abide. Could not relaxify into respectability. (140)

Wideman goes on to expose the contradiction inherent in of Miranda's stance. Her righteous indignation at Caliban's vulgar invitation does nothing to challenge Prospero's similar desire to "Xerox" himself by using Miranda's body as a copy machine. Prospero and Caliban have more in common than either would care to admit. Thus we arrive at the play's subtext as Wideman reads it: "Spirit needs flesh. Word needs deeds" (141). In Wideman's revision of Shakespeare, Prospero's rise to power, then, is clearly won by alternately exploiting and thwarting the reproductive function of other characters including Miranda and her absent mother as well as Sycorax, Caliban, and his absent father.

While Baker and Wideman seem to sympathize with Caliban, the difficulty for the black woman who is trying to read this text is not in identifying with the distorted figure of Caliban but in finding kinship with Sycorax whose alienation presents itself as the opposite of "rootedness." After all, Baker's efforts in *Modernism* are to use notions of family to ground himself within an academic tradition. And if, both the African American male readers naturally identify with the "witch's whelp" then the African American female reader struggles to imagine that others see her as Sycorax or to imagine herself in Sycorax's place. *"Let's face it,"* as Hortense *Spillers maintains, "I am a marked woman, but not everybody knows my name. 'Peaches' and 'Brown Sugar,' 'Sapphire' and 'Earth Mother,' 'Aunty,' 'Granny,' God's 'Holy Fool,' a 'Miss Ebony First,' or 'Black Woman at the Podium': I describe a locus of confounded identities, a meeting ground of investments and privations in the national treasury of rhetorical wealth"* (65). "Peaches" and "Brown Sugar," fine, but I am no "Earth Mother" or "Granny." I am more confined than Spillers. Holloway describes the nature of discrimination against black women in these terms:

> *Because sexism does not separate itself from the ethics of racism, the relationship between gender and ethnicity follows established stratifications within society. Foucault's suggestion that the bodies of individuals are vulnerable to the operations of power help to clarify the notion that as long as bodies are distinguished in political and social systems in terms of ethnicity and gender, these*

> *bodies can be even more carefully distinguished (the aim of prejudice is finer and finer forms of distinction) by another level of bias. In light of this claim, "blackwoman" can be conceived of as a category in the same way that "black" and "woman" are social categories. (4)*

My experiences affirm this logic; I find myself constrained by increasingly smaller categories. Even while on campus only people who know address me as a professor. To everyone else I am: Ma'am. Ms. Miss. Young Lady. Honey. Sweetheart. Baby. Sister Girl. Woman. Red Bone! Yallow!! JEZEBEL!!!

In the mid-twentieth century African American women were finally able to enter the academic intercourse in significant numbers, where identity matters are fertile ground for a bountiful crop of intellectual labor. Although African American women entering the academy had been liberated from the economics of slavery many of the dynamics at work in the formative stages of the development of their identity were still working to draw them into a complex set of negotiations. These negotiations demonstrated that African American women scholars remained in a precarious position that largely reflected pre-existing racial and sexual power relationships. Under the illogic of the plantation economy African American women were subjected to white male libidinous desire irrespective of biological ties. In the slave system a (white) man could literally and figuratively increase his stock by reproducing and subsequently denying natural bonds of kinship in favor of the bounds of chattel slavery. Consequently, the African American female identity, conceived in the hull of a slave ship traversing the Middle Passage, spent her maidenhood in the Antebellum South under the watch of a rapacious father. The dis-ease produced by this unique set of circumstances was not remedied by the dismantling of slavery.

Even after African American women began exercising agency in the intellectual debate, black female identity seemed to be formulated in capitulation to or reaction against this troubled history but it was hardly imagined apart from the legacy of slavery. In this chapter, I unpack what Michel Foucault might call the "system of alliance" that makes kin of intellectuals and scholars in order to reveal a troubled family narrative. Take, for example, the work of Pulitzer Prize winning playwright, Suzan-Lori Parks. Parks insists on bringing the vernacular and often mundane experiences of African Americans to the stage and in so doing, she carries on the legacy of Zora Neale Hurston (which I discuss in the second chapter). While Hurston's efforts to document and create unselfconsciously black art were frustrated by the sexism and racism of her day, Parks' relative social privilege allows her to do so more freely. Nevertheless, Parks' individual liberty does not demonstrate a wholesale transformation of a culture that has historically defined black women in the marketplace in terms of the service they perform with their bodies. Historically, Saartjie (pronounced Sar-key) Baartman, pejoratively called the Hottentot Venus better illustrates the way black women enter academic intercourse. Baartman's distinguishing feature for the European scientific community that exploited her for nearly two centuries was her really large butt. Baartman serves as the sign of black womanhood, as the very embodiment of phallic lack—a lack of knowledge, a lack of intellect, of dignity, of respect, of desire, a lack of power, a lack of humanity.

Despite the academy's continued investment in seeing black women as the Hottentot Venus, initially African American women entered academic intercourse as subject by representing themselves as "daughter." Toni Morrison, Gayl Jones, Maya Angelou, Alice Walker, Toni Cade Bambara, Gloria Naylor, Ntozake Shange, and others tell stories within the context of the family of girls crossing the difficult threshold of womanhood. Scholars like Barbara Smith, Nellie McKay, Ann du Cille, Gloria Hull, Barbara Christian, Hazel Carby, Valerie Smith, Karla Holloway, and Deborah McDowell supported the literary merit of this burgeoning "sisterhood" of African American women's writing. In the second portion of this three-part tale, I consider the position of this daughter. Rather than a beloved child, the daughter reveals through her stories the abuse she often receives at the hands of men. These stories put her into immediate conflict with the pre-existing "father's law" that governs the literary culture in which these women are participating.

I bring the issue of male privilege to the foreground by juxtaposing a reading of Michael Awkward's memoir, which tells the story of how he comes to be a feminist scholar, with the story of Violet, one of my former students. Awkward builds the story of his academic journey around his mother's body. However, the troubled history that Awkward displaces onto his mother's body, Violet (and Awkward's mother) must experience in her own. Like Awkward, Violet is a first generation college student who struggles to acquire an academic veneer. The "father's law" that dictates so much of our academic behavior is more potent than the presence of Violet's actual father and the absence of Awkward's, and their stories demonstrate the ways that even a sympathetic son nonetheless can be subsumed under the authority of the "father's law."

Inheritance

Once pon time. As that fancy one dere dose testify. Mine by way Queen Sycorax my mother. Him say all dat and say my mother am witch. Why him play dozens now? Say island belong to him now. Say my mother dead in nother country. Why he swoop down like great god from the sky, try make everybody feel high? Take ebryting. Den ebryting give back. Go off teach at University. Write book. Host talk show. Jah self don't know what next dis dicty gentleman do.

> Ebryting restore but what him first stole. Island mine from my poor mother. Island stole from me.
>
> Noting make self. I be her son and son of some fader. Don't try guess who. Don't say in de play. I no know, no want to know. Just want island back. Queen Mama back. No time be playing dozens now.
>
> —John Edgar Wideman, *Philadelphia Fire*

Inconsiderate vents kept coughing out hot breaths of steam despite the unseasonably mild New England winter. The additional heat generated by too many bodies in one room only compounded my discomfort. A nun who habitually attended lectures hosted in and around Harvard Square packed herself in the seat beside me. Although we spoke with our mouths averted to avoid breathing into one another's faces, we managed to have a friendly conversation. Familial obligations kept me home most of the time but every so often I would board a flight and make my way to Cambridge. I was glad that on this occasion Suzan-Lori Parks would be here to speak. In 2002 Parks became the first African American woman to receive the Pulitzer Prize for drama and I appreciated the uncompromising voice with which she spoke through her work.

Although I'd never seen her before I recognized her immediately in this crowd of strangers. Parks has the look of someone familiar with the stage. Her girlish frame draped in thick, coal black locks, as if let down from Rapunzel's tower. But her eyes, rimmed in heavy black liner said, "I'll climb down my own ropes of hair—thank you—and free myself." She dressed simply in a black T-shirt with a pair of worn jeans. Although Parks was here to address an audience of some of the nation's best and brightest, she was not pressed. She stood out from the rest of us who in one way or another fell into conventions even as we swam up stream. Unfortunately, like salmon we were seeking a place to drop some eggs and die. Parks, on the other hand, did not have the flushed pallor of one bloated with want and desire.

After her talk I went up to introduce myself and to have my book signed but people kept cutting in front of me like I wasn't there. When I finally became annoyed and voiced my frustration the woman with whom I had been chatting said, "At least there's only one door and she can't get out without coming past us." I smiled and agreed that as long as I was able to speak with her before she left, I was okay. Just after I shook hands with Suzan-Lori and began to tell her how much I identified with parts of her discussion, Professor Howard Rhodes who was to escort her to dinner walked up and told her it was time to go. I didn't have time to bristle my feathers before she set some boundaries, "Wait a minute!" Then to me she asked in a decidedly more patient tone, "What is your name?"

"Her name is Willy!" Professor Rhodes said. I had no idea why someone of such obvious intelligence would behave so badly. I saw him

looking smug and satisfied over my right shoulder before she and I agreed without words that it was his turn to be invisible. Neither she nor I acknowledged his intrusion and we decided that at least for the moment, we would not recognize him at all. I told her my name. We spoke for minute or so longer before she removed the top from her sharpe. I already owned copies of Venus *and* Top Dog/Underdog *and following her talk I bought* The America Play and other Stories. *But it was my copy of* The Red Letter Plays *that I handed her to sign, which she did in bold lettering: "For Valerie S L Parks" decorated with hearts and a star.*

Parks' *Red Letter Plays* revise Nathaniel Hawthorne's *The Scarlet Letter*. Hawthorne's Hester Pryne becomes Hester La Negrita of *In the Blood* and Hester Smith in *Fucking A*. Parks replaces Hawthorne's stark Puritan New England with the destitution of urban blight. Parks's protagonists are illiterate and impoverished Black women who are exploited and abused. Nearly everyone views Hester's victimization as inherent to her condition. The plays depict the protagonists at their most tragic moments, when the world around them becomes completely unbearable and they are finally dehumanized. Hawthorne's Hester must wear the scarlet letter to identify her as an adulterer; Parks's Hester's "crimes" are more evident. The red letter "A" in both cases is drawn in blood, the first in the blood of the son she kills in her frustration and despair and in the other, in the oozing bloody letter branded to label her as an abortionist. Parks's revisions of *The Scarlet Letter* critique the modern welfare state that encourages women to rely upon disinterested government programs without offering them a viable means of escaping the cycle of poverty. Moreover, *In the Blood* and *Fucking A* bring the black woman's reproductive function into public intercourse by making it central to the action of the play.

The Prologue for *In the Blood* begins with the cast "clustered together" and emphatically expressing their disdain for Hester La Negrita:

ALL: THERE SHE IS!
    WHO DOES SHE THINK
    SHE IS
    THE NERVE SOME PEOPLE HAVE

> SHOULDNT HAVE IF YOU CANT AFFORD
> IT
> AND YOU KNOW SHE CANT
> SHE DONT GOT NO SKILLS
> CEPT ONE
> CANT READ CANT WRITE (5)

This opening immediately depicts the contested role the black female protagonist has within the public marketplace. Hester has earned the contempt of society primarily because she is poor, illiterate, and she has five children with five different fathers. Her fertility reinforces rather than diminishes her apparent worthlessness. Reproduction, in the case of La Negrita, is not perceived as productive. Instead the poor, ignorant black woman apparently lives off the productivity of others. Her sexuality is the ultimate demonstration of her limitless potential to drain a vital society.

Hester La Negrita lives with her children under a bridge where someone has scribbled the epithet "SLUT" on a wall. Hester relies on her oldest son, Jabber, to read the graffiti. The word has been written in the place Hester practices writing the alphabet—which she stops after the first letter, repeatedly writing the letter "A." Jabber tries to lessen the significance of the word by pretending he can't read it. Hester suspects that he can read the word and that it upset him but Jabber dismisses its impact by insisting, "Words don't hurt my feelings, Mamma" (12). "Sticks and stones," he suggests without completing the rhyme. In the end, of course, it will be a billy-stick wielded by his frustrated and rejected mother that will kill him.

    Hester's love for her children is strained by their circumstances. Nevertheless she does her best to offer them a wholesome life. Unfortunately, the only resource available to Hester is a retreat into fantasy. And stories do little to put meat on their bones. The thin familiar soup she serves the children "is a very special blend of herbs and spices. The broth is chef Mommies worldwide famous 'whathaveyou' stock. Theres carrots in there. Theres meat. Theres oranges. Theres pie" (17). She feeds her children hope by telling these stories. Some are fantasies woven around Hester's memories of their fathers. In reality, Hester has little control over their well-being or her own. She is hungry and the children are not well cared for. Even the Doctor sexually exploits her and wants to rid her of her "womanly parts" so that he and others like him can continue to do so with impunity. While Hester is exploited bodily by nearly everyone she encounters, the children's illusive fathers are able to avoid the welfare system as if they are really as fanciful as her stories make them out to be. Without genuine assistance, Hester has no idea how to gain control over her life.

In *Fucking A*, Parks transforms the unskilled Hester La Negrita into Hester Smith who performs a useful service for society. After Hester Smith finds a choice piece of meat on her doorstep she wonders if someone might be trying to poison her but her friend, Canary, explains, "No one would wanna kill you. We need you too much. Like me, you perform one of those disrespectable but most necessary services" (121). Canary is a kept-woman, to whom the Mayor *owns* "exclusive rights," and Hester is an abortionist. Like Hester La Negrita, these two women are part of the class of people who are forced to live off their wit and bodies. Hester Smith has been giving every spare dime to

Freedom Fund to buy her son's release from prison. Hester will never be able to stop paying into this system which is designed to keep Hester as well as her son complacent by making false promises of an impending release.

Years ago, Hester "[s]crubbed floors for the Rich Family" but she became an abortionist after her son, Boy, was incarcerated for stealing meat from them. Hester still holds the Little Rich Girl responsible for his imprisonment because she told her parents. "You cant blame her for his current incarceration," Freedom Fund insists. "His initial three year sentence has doubled and tripped and quadrupled and—since hes been in jail hes committed several crimes" (134). Hester's "motherlove" only allows her to see her son as an "angel." In fact, Boy Smith is Monster, the escaped convict three Hunters have been tracking throughout the play. Motherlove, like the kind Paul D describes to Sethe in Toni Morrison's *Beloved* as "too thick," distorts her judgment to the point that she is willing to "eat" her son. She bites his arm to mark him and gives herself the same mark in an effort to guarantee that she will recognize him when she sees him again. She describes the scene:

> Hester: When they comed to take him away, just before they took him, I bit him. Hard. Right on the arm just here. I bit hard. Deep into his skin. His blood in my mouth. He screamed but then he was screaming anyway. After theyd took him away I went and bit myself. Just as hard and in the same place exactly. See the mark I got? My Boys got one too. Identical.
>
> *She shows him [Butcher] her bite mark scar, on the inside of her left forearm, the remains of a horrid wound.* (166)

While Hester sees the mark as evidence of her motherly devotion it is more clearly a demonstration of a desperate woman's attempt to exert control in a situation over which she has little power. The power she does have is to hurt herself or her young son, in effect reflecting his theft in a ghastly distortion. Boy satisfied his hunger by stealing meat; Hester does likewise.

However, the poverty of her environment does not encourage her to perceive her actions as transgressive. No one cares if Hester eats Boy alive. In fact, Rich Family and Freedom Fund are content to have him languish in prison for the rest of his life.

When Hester is finally able to come up with enough money to get Freedom Fund to arrange a picnic lunch meeting with her son, they have no idea where he is. In place of her son the prison guards callously send another convict to picnic. The convict is ravenous and eats like an animal before he notices Hester's attention:

    Jailbait: Yr looking at me like you wanna eat me up.

    Hester: Motherlove. (180)

Despite their time apart, Hester's desire toward her son is still consuming. Her love for him is cannibalistic and she is unable to draw healthy boundaries between them. It's the kind of love that might lead a mother like Eva Peace in Toni Morrison's *Sula* to hold her son "real close" before setting him on fire, trying to keep him from crawling back into her womb. But Jailbait distorts Hester's "motherlove" into sexual desire.

Jailbait puts his head in her lap suggesting the image of the Pieta but soon the image of the Virgin Mother is perverted as it transforms into a scene of rape. When Hester objects to his initial physical advances, Jailbait asserts, "Yr not no virgin are you?" (182) as he proceeds to defile her. When she doesn't see the scar she made on Boy's arm, Hester realizes that Jailbait is not her son and she lacks the will to fight him off. As the scene closes Hester appears like Jezebel, alternately Madonna and a whore.

The chorus in the Prologue of *In the Blood* suggests that if Hester La Negrita had a husband she would be released from her social caste. In this play, Hester Smith has a suitor who is an honest working man. Butcher loves Hester and wants to marry her; however, she is reluctant to marry him. Throughout, the comparison between Butcher and Hester is obvious. Their bloody aprons suggest daily slaughter. For a butcher, death and life are interconnected; the meat from the butcher block provides food for the table. Butcher explains:

> Butcherings the only thing I ever wanted to do. I feel like Im right

> in the middle of the great chain of being. Passing life from one group to another. Sure I kill them but I make sure it never hurts. Ive spent all my life perfecting the painless slaughter. (162)

Perhaps this is why Butcher initially offers to teach Hester to read and write but winds up teaching her a technique for killing without pain. This is the technique Hester Smith uses when she, like Hester La Negrita, kills her son.

When Hester finally encounters her son, she does not recognize him. Her mark looks like a heart to her while his looks like a horrible gash. She fails to recognize the "Monster" she's produced. Hester does not recognize Monster as her son until she's taken revenge on the Little Rich Girl, who's grown up to be First Lady as the Mayor's wife. After many years, First Lady has finally conceived a child. The Mayor celebrates his anticipated heir. But Hester has her drugged and performs an abortion on her. What she doesn't realize is that she has aborted her own grandchild—the clear evidence of the Mayor's sterility and her own fertility—conceived during a brief affair between First Lady and her fugitive son. Hester's long awaited reunion with her son is tragically short as he begs her to kill him rather than allow the Hunters who are in close pursuit to catch him alive. Ultimately, Hester's bloody employment becomes her undoing as she slaughters both her son and his seed.

In *The Red Letter Plays*, Hester's creative outlets are reduced to reproduction and murder. In telling the story of the illiterate, impoverished black woman, Parks embodies society's outcasts in both language and form, authorizing their inclusion in the academic intercourse. Parks explains her philosophy:

> A play is a blueprint of an event: a way of creating and rewriting history through the medium of literature. Since history is a recorded or remembered event, theatre, for me, is the perfect place to "make" history—that is, because so much of African American history has been unrecorded, dismembered,

> washed out, one of my tasks as playwright is to—through literature and the special strange relationship between theatre and real-life—locate the ancestral burial ground, dig for bones, find bones, hear the bones sing, write it down. ("Possession" 4)

Such a philosophy places history under the management and authorial control of the playwright. For Parks, history is the embodiment of the past in the present. Once Parks liberates herself from chronological constraints and sees the past, as Deborah McDowell describes it, "as a function of a continuous present," she is able to move freely through not only time and space. Both time and space, then, function as discourse available for Parks's skillful crafting.

Her masterful negotiation of the "special strange relationship between theatre and 'real life' *place* her within the present performance even as it works discursively to remove her from material limitations. Playwriting becomes more than a simple memorial. It functions as a ceremonial retrieval, a way of calling back and giving new life to that which seemed irretrievably lost—at least so long as the play is performed. The play and the playwright are lent as vessels, immersed in the ancient African act of ritual possession. As Baker notes, "In specifically diasporic terms, 'being possessed' (as slave, but also as a BEING POSSESSED) is more than a necessary doubling or inscribed 'otherness' of the *con-scripted* (those who come, as necessity, *with* writing). For in the diaspora, the possessed are governed not simply by *script* but also by productive conditions that render their entire play a *tripling*" (53). The spirits of dead ancestors, whose bones are buried in unmarked graves, have names that are lost to memory and must be unearthed, dug up, in Parks's conception, from the "Great Hole in History." History is a sort of possession—the past taking over a body for the purpose of "re-membering" in a way that Toni Morrison suggests in *Beloved*.

Although these "remembered" voices are mediated by Parks as the playwright they remain essentially vernacular. In the modern academic world, African American vernacular has found a place within the high culture of deconstruction.

Scholars discuss African American vernacular using the language of literary theory. However, in representing the vernacular experiences of the urban African American female underclass while working in the tradition of the theatrical *avant-garde,* Parks reinforces the importance of shifting from the linguistic concern with the signifier to that of the material body, the signified. By "digging" into the 'Great Hole in History," Parks reconfigures Baker's "black (w)holes"— transforming his extraterrestrial metaphor into one that is terrestrial and preoccupied with inner spaces and the body. The vernacular, manifested in Parks's first novel, *Getting Mother's Body,* as a search for the black mother, circles back on itself and uncannily it becomes indistinguishable from the quintessential African American experience of being ruthlessly un-mothered. The antebellum assertion that a child follow the condition of the mother effectively denied black people human rights. Ties to the mother were used to justify the enslavement of future generations. So expression of the vernacular is a defiant effort to demonstrate the connection one has to the mother in the face of overwhelming opposition working to deny that very bond.[5]

In some ways, expressions of the vernacular within the context of black America become a sophisticated manifestation of counter culture. If the dominant culture seeks to assimilate the citizenry through the process of public education, then the vernacular is an effort to maintain a distinct cultural identity. The vernacular represents a determination to ground oneself and to reaffirm ones connection to the mother as an originary source. In its most common practice, the black vernacular demonstrates an obsessive focus on "Yo' Mama!"—as if these two words when uttered with the right inflection say all there is to say about who we are in relationship to one another. Yet somehow the focus of the joke seems to always be on *your* mother rather than mine. It affirms ones birthright even as it seeks to denigrate native ties. The attachment is, of course, mythical, recalling the Yoruba goddess Odu who carries an enigmatic calabash[6] that is the primal matrix for all the stories in the world.

That evening while I sat in that room in Cambridge, Parks read from some of her work and shared her motivation for writing a play based on the life of Saartjie Baartman, the Hottentot Venus. Baartman voluntarily left her home in Cape Town, South Africa in 1810 to seek her fame and fortune as a performer. Her departure was motivated by William Dunlop, a naval doctor, who thought her distended backside might draw a crowd. When Baartman reached Europe, she could speak several languages. Nevertheless, she was forced to perform nearly naked in a cage as part of a freak show in Piccadilly, England. Overlooking her intelligence, ambition, and courage, Europeans paid to see Baartman's black butt. The efforts of abolitionists who sought to free her from this life of public humiliation were thwarted by Baartman's testimony that she was a willing participant in this exhibition with a share of the profits.

Later, Baartman was sold to a French entrepreneur who brought her to Paris where she was studied for scientific evidence of the mythic "Hottentot apron," a physical marker reported by European travelers to confirm the Khoisan woman's sexual and racial difference.

As Baartman's biographer, Rachel Holmes, asserts:

> *There was a typical colonial contradiction about black female sexuality at the heart of how travelers and scientists imagined the 'Hottentot apron'. It was seen to signify the notion that Khoisan women were simultaneously uncontrollably libidinous and coyly modest. Whether a result of nature or nurture, the apron, it was believed, functioned to conceal and contain excessive sexuality and deviant desires. In time-honored tradition, the virgin and the whore were rolled into one. (142)*

After her untimely death in 1816, anatomist Georges Curvier dissected her labia and presented it to the Academie Royale de Medecin as an explanation for the African woman's "primitive sexual appetite." Baartman's dismembered posterior and genitalia were given to La Musée de l'Homme and kept on display along with her skeleton until the mid 1970s. In the reductive reasoning of the French scientific community Baartman was literally reduced to meat and bones. Baartman's pickled parts were exhibited like those of a rare species and bore the weight of racial stereotypes about black women for nearly two hundred years. Late in the twentieth century, she became the focus of an international struggle waged by South Africa to bring her body home. In her lifetime, as Holmes notes, Baartman was "[f]ought over like disputed territory" (90), a dispute over territorial boundaries which remained unsettled well beyond her lifetime. Uncertain as to the response from various nations who might want to lay claim to other museum holdings, France was reluctant to turn over Baartman's remains. In April 2002, nearly two centuries after she left Cape Town, Baartman was finally dignified with a burial in her homeland.

South Africa's insistence on moving beyond mere memorial to the actual ceremonial retrieval of Baartman's remains is fundamentally a dispute over possession. South

Africa's claim on her body seeks to repudiate Western domination and the colonization of its people. Interring Baartman's material remains in her homeland reinforces South Africa's discursive claims on her story. The international squabble mirrors the academic contest as Black women strive to repossess Baartman's body after centuries of abuse in the hands of white, male discourse.

Although my husband had introduced me to Saartjie Baartman some time ago, the experience of sitting in a sweltering room in Cambridge reflecting on the nineteenth century "discovery" of Baartman's butt was disconcerting, not only because of the absolute absurdity of the "scientific" conclusions but because this is literally and figuratively where I entered the academic intercourse. I had traveled hundreds of miles up the eastern seaboard to find that I have been carrying the Hottentot Venus on my back. I have been carrying her around like Pilate Dead's green sack of bones in Song of Solomon. *Baartman is my inheritance. I am not certain even now if we have laid all her bones to rest. I remember in my youth, before*

Baartman was buried, how we identified whether a girl was black or white. Everyone knew that flat and wide butts belonged to white girls, while fat and protruding butts were black. As teenagers we saw the backside as a repository for the black, female essence. And apparently no small container could hold all that. The butt mattered to us as kids and although these youthful fantasies have long since been displaced by less crude formulations of the black woman's body her backside still figures prominently in academic discussions about race and sex. Even if obscured by the ivy covering the walls, a ghost image remains of Baartman's bones, which hung for so long from the rafters.

The lecherous gaze of the academy has long been fixed on the black, female body. As Margaret Homans maintains, "in a world that binarizes into theory and examples, or mind and body, the black woman equals the body or the example" (75). At heart, many of the associations that troubled Baartman's treatment at the hands of the academy remain unresolved. Valerie Smith argues that black women are used as the ground upon which men and white women build their scholarship. Smith writes, "This association of black women with reembodiment resembles rather closely the association, in classic Western philosophy and in nineteenth-century cultural constructions of womanhood, of women of color with the body and therefore with animal passions and slave labor" (45). In " 'Women of Color' Writers and Feminist Theory," Homans picks up on Smith's argument and reads specifically the ways in which feminists (white and black) use black women to carry the weight of their arguments. Even across the gender divide male feminists similarly use the black woman's body. For example, Michael Awkward founds his identity as an African American feminist scholar upon the woman's body. In *Scenes of Instruction*, his memoir which I will say more about later, Awkward bares his mother's breasts and exclaims, "Ain't *I* a woman!"

Nanny, then, from Zora Neale Hurston's *Their Eyes Were Watching God* (1939) speaks with some insight when she declares, "De nigger woman is de mule uh de world so fur as Ah can see" (14). Nanny cannot see beyond the mechanisms set in place to limit black women's contributions to manual labor. Nanny exercises her modest power to direct her granddaughter, Janie, into a loveless marriage to a man who has enough economic resources to support her. Yet, the novel itself critiques the deployment of race and sex within a society that restricts the African American woman to her menial service to others. These restrictions are so severe for Nanny that from her perspective black women are reduced to beasts of burden. In the context of the academy as well, "De nigger woman *is* de mule uh de world so fur as Ah can see"—becoming the meat of academic service for the disembodied minds of those who write.

Hurston's novel and Parks's play, *Venus*, enter an intercourse that spans the African Diaspora within the academy where race and sex come together in an unholy union that is as troubled as it is potentially fruitful. These works arise in an era when black women are reclaiming their bodies and exerting more control over their reproductive capacities. Contemporary writers are catalyzed by the history of privation that led to the aborted careers and the malnourishment of black women authors like Nella Larsen and even

Zora Neale Hurston, both of whom died in obscurity. By making Baartman the subject of their work, Suzan-Lori Parks, Elizabeth Alexander, Barbara Chase-Riboud, Sandra Gilman, Londa Schlebinger, Jean Young, and others allow the Hottentot Venus to enter an intercourse around race and sex as subject rather than as a mere object of commerce. This engagement serves as a vital stage in the liberation of the black female identity from the denigrating hands of a white, male intellectual culture content to reduce the African American woman, either through metaphor or metonymy, to an ass.

Where does that leave me—an African American female professor? As Homi Bhabha claims, "cultural difference becomes a problem not when you can point to the Hottentot Venus, or to the punk whose hair is six feet up in the air.... It is as the strangeness of the familiar that it becomes more problematic... when the problem of cultural difference is ourselves-as-others, others-as-ourselves, that borderline" (72). The discourse around Baartman positions me at an intersection where eros, the body, race, and sex meet academic inquiry. With the mind claimed as white, male, and saturated in so much of our thinking about academic matters, the body is marked as black, female, and vacuous. The imagined distance between the mind and body can be interpreted as an incredibly vast expanse when presented on the one hand as transcendent, eternal ideals and on the other as the terrestrial, largeness of Baartman's butt. Even as we make ethical shifts away from outmoded racist and sexist ideologies, the figure of the African American female continues to be routinely required to do the intellectual dirty work.

According to the Greek tradition, differences within the academy are negotiated among a select population of men ranging only in age and experience. The classical, European academic paradigm is derived from pederasty. As Jane Gallops observes:

> A greater man penetrates a lesser man with his knowledge. The student is empty, a receptacle for the phallus; the teacher is the phallic fullness of knowledge. The fact that teacher and student

> are traditionally of the same sex but of different ages contributes to the interpretation that the student has no otherness, nothing different from the teacher, simply less. (*Thinking Through the Body* 43)

Despite a developing societal repugnance for men who engage boys in sexual intercourse, the pederastic paradigm itself has hardly been altered. For the moment, I would like to leave aside questions that have become the focus of so much attention and public scrutiny about the potential for exploitation in a context that sanctions sexual intercourse between adults and children. Instead, I want to point out a more neglected consequence of our continued investment in this paradigm.

The dichotomy established between teacher and student is very often that of phallic knowledge and prone receptacle. The professor inseminates the student with his knowledge, leaving him "pregnant" with possibility. When we utilize terms like "phallus" deriving from psychoanalysis we invoke the work of Freud and

Jacques Lacan, of course, but we can also look to the scholarship of intellectuals dominant in African American studies including W. E. B. Du Bois, Henry Louis Gates, and Houston Baker who deliberately engage in discussions about race and to some degree gender yet continue to follow the classic tradition. In *Race Men*, Hazel Carby offers a critique of the African American male intellectual model that effectively functions to displace the female body. Carby writes:

> The map of intellectual mentors [Du Bois] draws for us [in *Souls of Black Folk*] is a map of male production and reproduction that traces in its form, but displaces through its content, biological and sexual reproduction. It is reproduction without women, and is a final closure to Du Bois's claim to be "flesh of the flesh and bone of the bone," for in the usurpation of the birth of woman from Adam's rib, the figure of the intellectual and race leader is born of and

engendered by other males. (25-6)

The introduction of women into the academy does not necessitate the disruption of the paradigm. As Carby notes, "The failure to incorporate black women into the sphere of intellectual equality... is not merely the result of the sexism of Du Bois's historical moment... It is a conceptual and political failure of imagination that remains a characteristic of the work of contemporary African American male intellectuals" (10).

Even when the male titans of the field of African American studies acknowledge phallocentricism, they have done little to dismantle its authority. Instead, their work actively reinforces the symbolic power of the phallus and its discursive tyranny. In fact, the black female body is coopted and used within the institutional framework to reinforce the illusion of masculine power by expanding the pedagogical terrain. Her body is another site of potential invasion. Furthermore, given the physical absence of a penis and her exaggerated girth, the African American female body is the quintessential receptacle. Unlike the male student who is "simply less" than the pederast in Gallop's terms, the African American woman is "essentially" different. Her backside as the container of her black womaness is so incredibly huge that one can hardly imagine it ever being filled. Consequently she is not permitted to shift at some ripe moment from the effeminized position of student to the phallicized position of the teacher. In this formulation, she can never be the pederast because she embodies phallic lack. I don't mean to suggest that this is altogether a bad thing. Why should I ever want to be a pederast? But if this is the model that shapes the profession for me, then it must be interrogated—the good, the bad, and the down right obscene.

Perhaps Toni Morrison is right in suggesting in *Sula* that if you stir a man's mind, you stir his body. The scene to which I am referring appears after the title character returns to the Bottom. Sula is visiting her best friend when Nel's husband comes in from work complaining about his treatment at the hands of the white man. The novel reads:

Sula was smiling. "I mean, I don't know what the fuss is about. I mean, everything in the world loves you. White men love you. They spend so much time worrying about your penis they forget their own.... And if that ain't love and respect I don't know what is. And white women? They chase you all to every corner of the earth, feel for you under every bed.... Now ain't that love?... Colored women worry themselves into bad health just trying to hang on to your cuffs.... And if that ain't enough, you love yourselves. Nothing in this world loves a black man more than another black man. You hear of solitary white men, but niggers? Can't stay away from one another a whole day. So it looks to me like you the envy of the world."

> Jude and Nel were laughing.... A funny woman, [Jude] thought, not that-bad-looking. But he could see why she wasn't married; she stirred a man's mind maybe, but not his body. (103-4)

In the next paragraph we find Nel confronting her husband's absence. Two paragraphs later we discover why Jude is gone. Nel has discovered Jude with her best friend, Sula, having sex on the floor "like dogs." And thus Morrison highlights the fallacy of Jude's earlier reasoning. The novel implies: if you stir a man's mind then you stir his body.

In fact, minds and bodies are not separate from one another; they are quite obviously connected. As Gallop has properly noted, "The phrase 'mind-body split' connotes appropriately metaphysical abstraction, even though it poses the fundamental question of and to metaphysics. But... we think physically rather than meta-physically, if we think the mind-body split *through the body*, it becomes an image of shocking violence" (*Thinking Through the Body*

1). The trouble is that we seek to deny the obvious in favor of what we believe to be "higher" ideals. We may be able to repress the basic truth of such connections for some time but, as Jude discovers, when the contradiction surfaces the consequences may be dire. His baser instincts prevail and not only does Jude succumb, but as Nel's description demonstrates his act is hardly distinguishable from that of an animal. To stir a man's mind *is* to stir his body.

I feel the need to reassert the obvious—minds are not separate from bodies. Consider, for example, the fact that the word "seduction" shares the Latin root of "education." I am offended by the great privilege implied by questions asked by philosophers like Jacques Lyotard who muses, "Can thought go on without a body?" Why are we so invested in such a split? What will happen if we resist the urge to make the mind distinct from the body? Perhaps we may be able to demystify the tensions at work in the classroom and in the office that can be so problematic at times. After all, the principles that led to abstracting the mind from the body are evident in the classical tradition that linked pedagogy and pederasty.

Reflect on *The Symposium* written by Plato who is recognized as the father of Western thought. This dialogue illustrates social interaction among the elite class of Greece. It is named after the room built into the homes of the aristocracy where men gathered to enjoy food, wine, and the pleasure of one another's company. According to *The Symposium* the ideal pedagogical model couples an older, wiser man with a ripe, intelligent adolescent boy. Plato distinguishes between the body, identified by physical lust, and the soul that desires a more transcendental relationship. The soul is masculine, intangible, noble, and cerebral. *The Symposium* begins with a discussion of sexual desire that establishes the terms of the relationship between master and pupil as a male, homosexual dynamic between asymmetrical powers. Their mutual desire to stimulate the mind is also expressed bodily through sex.

For many scholars like William Armstrong Percy, III pederasty is equated with a vibrant intellectual culture. His study *Pederasty and Pedagogy in Archaic Greece* is respected for documenting the enduring influence of the institution of pederasty as a pedagogical practice in ancient Greece. In addition to helping to curtail population growth, pederasty was an effective way of inculcating the next generation of military and civic leaders. Percy accepts wholeheartedly the values perpetuated by this ancient institution and writes nostalgically about its loss. Boys were trained to serve the needs of the state; meanwhile, girls were taught to serve as wives and mothers. In an effort to dismiss the obvious bias toward men inherent in the institution, Percy points to the ancient poet Sappho whose work seems to suggest a female pederastic model. He writes, "Although this study is concerned with (male) pederasty, Sappho's poetry must be mentioned since it represents such a clear parallel in the world of females to cardinal features of Greek pederastic practices" (Percy 147). Unfortunately, in alluding to Sappho Percy does not apply his characteristic attention to scholarly detail.

Sappho wrote at the end of the seventh century B. C. E. on the island of Lesbos and was regarded by Plato as the tenth muse. Her work has long been cited as the earliest example of a western woman's writing. The lack of biographical detail, the fragmentary remains of her poetry, the homoeroticism suggested by her verses, as well as her reported suicide over unrequited love fuel her legendary status. For centuries, scholars have constructed a mythology around this ancient figure as a mistress of a school for girls. She has been imagined to fit within the broader masculine social framework. But this is problematic, as Holt Parker observes through carefully tracing the history of scholarship about Sappho:

> Chronologically, the earliest witness (Horace) is six hundred years after Sappho. As evidence the testimonies are valueless, again turning poetry into biography. They do not prove that Sappho ran a school. They do not prove that Sappho loved only nubile girls. What they do show is something quite familiar to feminists: the wholesale

> restructuring of female sexuality
> and society on the model of male
> sexuality and society. (158)

In flattening his reading of Sappho's poetry into his argument about the value and contribution of pederasty, which concern only the desires of men, Percy overlooks important distinctions.

In this ancient culture, a woman's potential was limited by her reproductive capacity. The natural reproductive function performed by women was considered debased and as a result they were left to tend the private needs of the family. Women were not permitted to engage in the symposia and other arenas where learning took place. Her intellectual capacity, then, appeared to be limited by her reproductive function. In order for women to become equal with men in their intellectual capacity Plato argues in his most famous dialogue, *The Republic,* they must be liberated from their "private" function within the family. Since academic work is separated from the work of the family, the female scholar also must be perceived apart from her reproductive function.

In *The Symposium,* women do not contribute to the conversation until Socrates speaks late in the dialogue. The woman, Diotima, is spoken into existence through the all-wise, philosopher-teacher Socrates. Ostensibly, it is Diotima who educates Socrates on love. While Socrates suggests that he learns from her, everyone else both inside and outside the text learns from Socrates since Diotima is not present in her material body. She enters as a maternal figure who helps to translate Socrates's reading of love from physical sex to a metaphor of reproduction that liberates sexuality (which is codified as love) from the physical body.

Nevertheless, the physical body played a significant role in the Greek academic tradition. Attractive adolescent boys were invited to eat and drink with men in the symposia where the former were seduced with wine, poetry, and song. Here boys were trained in the ways of upper class men. Since men often were restricted by law from marrying until thirty, they would take an adolescent as a lover. These youth were selected because of their potential to replicate the values esteemed by the intelligentsia. In this way, the male pedagogue searches for a "beautiful body" with whom he can "reproduce." Significantly, the metaphor connecting sex with the transmission of knowledge develops through the course of *The Symposium* into an image of a pregnant female who promises to give birth to "good sense" which leads naturally to justice and the wise rule of the state. The woman serves as a surrogate mother who carries wisdom for the man who can then abandon the literal process of reproduction in favor of the metaphor and raise his "offspring" absent of the degraded female body.

Interestingly, the process represented in *The Symposium* is replication rather than reproduction. In ancient Greece, an elder man was expected to literally share his virility by ejaculating in a youth. The student gained courage, wisdom, knowledge, and skill through intimate contact with his teacher. The teacher gained immortality by replicating himself in the form of his student. The younger generation learned by mirroring the behavior of their elders. After reaching adulthood, the student turned pederast, found a young lover of his own. The social space of Plato's academy is a male arena that is invested in both literal sex and figurative reproduction.

As a pedagogical institution, pederasty is inherently narcissistic. Plato uses his authority to restrict women within the space of the academy. Consequently, men have historically had power to participate and to forbid academic access to women, using a set of prescribed values as justification. Even without the physical act, sex remains intrinsic to the pedagogical model. Education relies upon a reproductive metaphor. The illusion of reproduction imitates the work of the body and usurps the role of women. Consequently, the homosocial world of men within an environment of higher education becomes implicitly a realm of (homo)sexual replication. This process explicitly works to reinforce characteristics already existing in the culture. Individuals are permitted access to the symposium because of their adherence to a set of known standards of age, beauty, social standing, gender, and intellect. Differences are not encouraged nor valued. The academy is founded on these principles.

Since the time of Plato, academics have been claiming similar authority to define the role women play. Women cannot be substituted for men in the pederastic equation and yield the same results. Rather, the system establishes and maintains a social hierarchy that privileges men. Without careful consideration, scholars will continue replicating existing systems of power. Take, for example, Holt Parker's rationale about the persistent reading of Sappho as a schoolmistress:

> To a large extent, I believe it is precisely this reinscription [of her within a pederastic model] that accounts for the extraordinary power of Sappho Schoolmistress over the imaginations of so many, despite the total lack of evidence for it... the model is of controlling male to controlled Other, and reveals a disturbing obsession with power and hierarchy. Sappho, the female poet, is being assimilated

as much as possible to the male, in order to neutralize her. (159)

The critical apparatus has demonstrated an overwhelming bias toward men who reinforce this Greek tradition. Women are coopted into this system.

The material presence of women who produce actual flesh and blood born children disrupts Plato's homosocial order. Pederasty has been used to reinforce the illusion of neat divisions between the mind as the province of men and the body as the realm of women. But the consequence of such an image as Jane Gallop notes is disturbing; "The mind-body split makes the mother into an inhuman monster by dividing the human realm of culture, history, and politics from the realm of [sensual] love, and the body where mother carries, bears, and tends her children" (*Thinking Through the Body* 2).

Although Suzan-Lori Parks is obviously some distance removed from Ancient Greece, philosophy as it has given rise to our current academic practice is generally attributed to Plato. Plato still figures as "father" for a playwright and professor like Parks. Within a contemporary context that resists work that does not reinforce particular notions of cultural superiority, African American playwrights are pressured to produce work that appeals to a narrowly defined "black" audience. This tradition seeks to ghettoize Parks and her work because she refuses to ascribe received notions of race and performance. Although Parks often had difficulty in her early career finding an appropriate venue for her more experimental plays, she managed to garner critical acclaim. However, she won the Pulitzer for her most traditional play, *Top Dog/Under Dog*, the story of two black brothers whose cons lead to fratricide. This fact, along with her forays into mainstream productions of screen plays for Spike Lee, Brad Pitt, and the reigning queen of daytime television, Oprah Winfrey, suggests something about the balancing act Parks performs in the service of her craft.

The thrust of her most recent work is not into the more enclosed discursive spaces of the academy, but outward into the broader marketplace. Parks's *365 Days 365 Plays* is, in her terms, an attempt to memorialize the "play" as a critical form capable of capturing the sentiment of *any* and *every* day through the ritual of writing and performance. The most remarkable aspect of these plays is her insistence that they be written and performed every day for what amounts to two years. She also has a very democratic philosophy of making them available to whoever wishes to produce them by issuing performance rights for as little as a dollar.

When confronted with overwhelming gaps in history, Parks consistently encourages us to dig into the present moment for those things that have passed. The "Great Hole" in history, then, will be amended by the flesh and blood of lived experiences that testify of another (very present) past that the absence—of bones, memorials, and history—denies. Parks tells us to memorialize mundane experiences and to perform them as a ceremonial retrieval that places the past in our possession. *"No!"* Parks exclaims, *"Thought does not go on without a body. We have to go get our mother's body. Dig her up. And let her speak." This, she insists, is our inheritance.*

omo-osu

> If language was my prison house, then writing was the wall over which I climbed for escape. But climbing the wall either way meant, finally, the same thing, and so language was the prison and the escape and therefore no prison at all, any more than freedom is confinement simply because it precludes one from being confined.
>
> —Percival Everett, *Glyph*

My first exposure to the type of intellectual production that characterizes the field of African American studies was the furor that erupted around Steven Spielberg's film adaptation of

Alice Walker's The Color Purple. *Although some thirty odd years have passed since the debate began in earnest over Ntozake Shange's choreopoem,* For Colored Girls Who Considered Suicide When the Rainbow is Enuf, *and it has been twenty years since Spielberg's film marked the flashpoint that brought the debate to the evening news and to my attention, I return to this spectacle because it marks for me the occasion when I became aware that intellectual work—that of novelists, critics, intellectuals, educators, academics—is fundamentally political. And at the epicenter of this work is a notion of family. For Alice Walker, family is a troubled concept that prompts sexual abuse and domestic violence; while for her critics, family is an idyllic notion of alliances connecting people of the African Diaspora. Even today the metaphor of family remains a vital part of African American intellectual production.*

When I first encountered this debate, I had yet to learn about the ways that power works beneath rhetoric and the image to complicate the plea for "racial unity" within a racist society. I did not realize at the time that the words "family" and "unity" were being used as an attempt to recuperate a social structure that sublimates the needs of black women and children to the desires of black men. By tying ourselves together in the loose associations of Africanist notions of kinship, African American men could claim authority as "father" beyond the space of their own home and family. They could justify their desire for power as a "natural right" although we had no blood ties. The language of kinship obscures the fact that beyond the segregationist practices of a white supremacist culture, African Americans have no "real" bonds at all.

Just when African American female expression was finally breaking free of the cultural restraints that kept it muffled in cookbooks, quilts, patches of garden, and tunes hummed for consolation, an angry outcry from inside this same culture arose in resistance. African American men and some women were angry about negative representations of black men. The New York Times Book Review, New York Times Magazine, Village Voice, *and other mainstream publications lent credence to the perception of a growing divide between African American men and women by keeping this debate in the public eye. Critics vehemently maintained that African American women, beginning with Ntozake Shange and culminating here with Alice Walker, were participating in a systematic attack upon black masculinity.*

By the time that I discovered Deborah McDowell's critique of the hullabaloo in a collection titled Changing Our Own Words, *the anthology was in its second edition and I was in graduate school. McDowell's essay, called appropriately enough, "Reading Family Matters" helped me utilize a broader vocabulary at a crucial time in my academic development. McDowell characterizes the controversy surrounding African American women's fiction, "a la Freud," as a family romance. She writes, "This family romance is de-romanticized in writings by the greater majority of black women. Text meets countertext, and the 'confrontation' might be described... as between the 'daughter's story and the father's law'" (78). The African American woman writer of the late twentieth century is "daughter" because she is literally and figuratively born out of an established literary patriarchy. Du Bois, Fitzgerald, Faulkner, Hemingway, Wright, and Ellison shaped the field for Shange, Morrison, Jones, and Walker. The "father's law" established by the tradition these men represent served as the bones that gave African American literature its structure. The law seemed to be inherent. Yet, the illusion of the father's law failed as an aesthetic device governing the African American canon.*

In Octavia Butler's Kindred *Dana's future is literally held captive in the past until her ancestor Rufus rapes Alice. Ursa, in Gayl Jones's* Corregidora *is born out of a legacy of incest and rape. Jones's* Eva's Man *begins with the title character dentally castrating her lover post-mortem—resolving in clear if gruesome terms the lingering question of the first novel, that the penis is meat rather than bone. Jim Trueblood and Matty Lou in* Invisible Man, *Celie in* The Color Purple, *Maya Angelou in* I Know Why the Caged Bird Sing, *Toni Morrison, Gloria Naylor, Ann Petry, Houston Baker, Ann du Cille,*

Hortense Spillers, artists and critics alike examine the intersection where these narratives converge. Historically, the father's law has made room for the kinds of atrocities that happen by restricting the kinds of stories the daughter is permitted to tell. Nevertheless, the father's law did not prove to be insurmountable and the women talked back.

McDowell historicized and exposed the anxiety expressed by this debate as the axis of power within African American studies began to expand and made room for more female voices. At a time when a conservative backlash sent the nation calling for "a return to family values" and black fatherhood stood out as a highly contested issue, African American men felt betrayed. Not because Walker had "lied" about harsh realities, but because she had shared the "truth" about the matter in such a public forum. I was sympathetic to their position. Yet I was troubled by the level of hostility expressed by the men toward this author. I was curious as to why men seemed to feel so personally indicted by a work of fiction. I was also curious about what fueled such high crime rates among African

American men. Many claimed that African American women were castrating black men, emasculating them to the point of death, but the rhetoric did not match the images airing nightly on the evening news. Black men were killing each other. All of this seemed to have a lot to do with notions of black masculinity and less to do with how African American women represented men in their work. Ultimately, I came to realize that the family ties at the heart of the debate are as mythical as the bond between Zeus and Athena.

Nevertheless, as a teenager, I adopted the prevalent language that labeled black men an "endangered species." It seemed crucial to me too, that we unite in support of our "brothers." We, meaning black women, should not do them any harm since so much had been done to us as black people. Although I liked The Color Purple *(the novel and to a lesser degree the film) and believed that an author had the right to tell her own story, there seemed to me a greater good at stake. I easily conflated the reading of literature and film with my own social context.*

I grew up with my family in the suburbs of Washington, D.C. During this time the city had the dubious distinction of the highest murder rate. D.C. was labeled the murder capital of the world—like murder was some kind of local delicacy packaged for export to the rest of the planet. African American boys and men were killing each other at an extraordinary rate. Crack cocaine had been introduced to the community with particularly catastrophic results. Weekend parties at local roller rinks were notorious for the up and down percussions of Go-Go bands whose volume seemed to be justified by the innumerable scantily clad girls bouncing through a reefer cloud into the arms of gun toting drug dealers. The music called and teenagers came from every direction despite the fact that before the night was over, one or two of them would likely be gasping for air in a pool of their own blood.

From my perspective, knowing the details of too many tragedies, the human cost in (male) blood clearly outweighed the desire for an honest (female) expression. No matter how "real" the tale was to Walker and the other women who were labeled "male bashers," I believed that they should see the potential for their stories to be co-opted for nefarious purposes. My overall perspective on the matter changed as I matured intellectually but at the time I believed that Walker should be silent if she could not tell a different story.

I sought to muzzle Walker like the fictitious Celie's step-father chooses to quiet her. "You better not never tell nobody but God" (1)— so Celie suffers abuse in silence at the hands of the men in her life. Celie's story breaks free of the bondage and isolation imposed upon her by this edict through letters written first to God and then to others. Celie is "spoiled" twice by the man she knew as her father. The children born of habitual rape are given away. Then she is pawned off into an abusive marriage. The revelation of her mother's remarriage is withheld from Celie until late in the novel. After the man she knows as her father dies, Celie inherits her childhood home. Although Walker does not mark him with the sin of a consanguine union, his position in the household as "father" makes the coupling read as incestuous.

Along with other African American women writers of the time, Walker draws upon the theme of incest as one of the most ghastly signs of the troubled African American family narrative. Hortense Spillers maintains that "fictions about incest provide an enclosure, a sort of confessional space for and between postures of the absolute, and in a very real sense it is only in fiction... that incest as dramatic enactment and sexual economy can take place at all" ("Permanent Obliquity" 128). In Spillers' terms, fictions about incest mediate between the absolute disconnectedness of the African American identity originating in the splitting apart of families during slavery and with the arbitrary designation of kinship that presents all African Americans as brothers and sisters connected by a shared history of struggle. The notion of incest is inserted between the extreme of alienation and the absolute of a common blood bond as the expression of a grotesque connectedness. In this way, incest becomes the perverse manifestation of a desire for pleasure and dominance so great that it satisfies itself at the expense of other needs. Fictions about incest disclose pain, expose the mechanisms of power, and hopefully by opening up a dialogue offer the potential for healing.

Take, for example, Ralph Ellison's Jim Trueblood who explains to the invisible man the dream that results in the impregnation of his eldest daughter. Despite the fact that he declares himself blameless because he acts as a result of a dream rather than with deliberate foresight, Trueblood claims, "a man can look at a little ole pigtail gal and see him a whore" (59). The basic nature of incest between a father and daughter, a man and "a little ole pigtail gal," is one of power inequities. The man sees the girl-child as a whore, a woman whose body is used as a commodity for men trafficking in pleasure. He creates the circumstances of the narrative by acting out his dream and he satisfies his desire for power and pleasure first through sexual intercourse with his daughter then on another level, through discursive intercourse with his audience of other men. On the one hand, the daughter is effaced either by an absolute disassociation from familial ties or through cathexis. On the other hand, Trueblood's confession unites a disparate audience into a "brotherhood." These improbable extremes, that of disassociation and brotherhood, are mediated by the morose logic of Trueblood's incestuous tale which draws our attention away from the illogic of his "family" structures to the immediate bodily expression of pleasure and pain.

Discussions of this scene ignited a mild firestorm within African American studies. If incest stood alone, then readers might be able to come to some agreement about how it should be interpreted. Instead, incest is part of an unsettling fusion of extreme disassociation, cathexis, brotherhood, and consanguine union. These terms transcend literature. They are bound up with an ideology of family that also permeates our critical apparatus.

Perhaps the most polarized readings of this scene come from Houston Baker and Ann du Cille. Du Cille attacks Baker for his willingness to read Trueblood's act as an attempt to establish a black, royal lineage. Baker writes, "The cosmic force of the phallus thus becomes, in the ritual action of the Trueblood episode, symbolic of a type of royal paternity, an aristocratic procreativity turned inward to ensure the royalty (the 'truth,' 'legitimacy,' or 'authenticity') of an enduring black line of descent" (*Blues Ideology* 183). Du Cille retorts, "To describe a father's sexual violation and impregnation of his daughter as 'an aristocratic procreativity turned inward' is to reduce not race to a trope, as Baker has elsewhere been accused of doing, but rape" (du Cille par 25). Baker's imposition of the phallus as a preeminent—"cosmic"—force reveals the lengths to which we are willing, in general, to impose a mythic black patriarch. The rape of a daughter is merely collateral damage in our search for the black father, the negative impact of his "cosmic" absence from society far greater than her (incidental) pain.

A young woman venturing onto these discursive grounds treads on treacherous territory. Take, for instance, my student Violet. Violet sought her degree as a means of transcending the cycle of poverty plaguing her community. "No one from back home," she claimed, "does anything." Drugs have ravaged what remains of the impoverished rural community where she was raised by her grandmother. She alone of the grandchildren made it to college. While Violet is no longer living with her aging grandmother who is still raising other people's children, she is not the educator she wants to be. Instead she finds herself abiding within a complex of back alleyways and detours that make up the contemporary academic cityscape. The move from the trailer in Violet's rural past to even the modest dwelling of a public school teacher is stymied by an indeterminate stay in her father's house.

I didn't want to visit Violet because I was afraid of being accused by the frustrations in Violet's life. "An education is an education!" I imagined her disappointments as angry screams. "Not opportunity! Not even hope! Just a series of lessons which make me unsuited to do the tasks I thought, by virtue of earning a degree, I would no longer be required to do." As a young woman starting in education, Violet's life mattered a lot to me. But I had the strong impression that I had let her down. And if I had failed to teach Violet something that had the power to change her life, then what had I done?

Some students simply cannot fulfill their "proper" roles. Domestic obligations often impede a student's academic career. Sometimes, students are unable to adopt the conventions of a particular discipline. For some social, psychological, and emotional needs remain unsatisfied by university life. For any number of reasons, these students fall out of step with the set of "hidden cues" established by the culture of the institution.

In some ways I was one of those students. Without deliberate intent, without even consciousness or understanding, I rejected many academic directives. For instance, I liked to translate the pompous jargon I found in our texts into narrative that, I imagined, would allow me to share my passion with my parents who were not academics. I substituted dramatic, performative expressions for the erudite vocabulary of my most beloved peers. Eventually, even my physical distance from campus mirrored the rhetorical distance already evident in my work. Now I can see that I tended to express myself in ways that frequently surprised my professors and threw them off their guard. At first, my remarks were taken as off-handed and initially, most of my professors did not take my input seriously. (My classmates were probably laying wages as to how long I would last in the program.) I found that I had to begin all of my graduate courses by demonstrating to my professors that I was qualified to participate in sophisticated discussions.

I rejected some of the unspoken tenets of our profession and in so doing, I positioned myself apart from the prescribed norms of the campus. In the process, in a way I drew my professors away from campus too. My behavior in the African American vernacular was "ghetto"—uncommon and somehow wrong. For instance, whenever one of my professors asked me, "Why do you study home?" I would respond with a story about my life and then I would say, "I feel like a slave girl." My home was closing in on me. I worked so hard to be independent and yet I felt trapped despite my best efforts. And for better or worse, this was all about home. My home.

My reply never failed to make my professor uncomfortable. He would say, "Don't respond like that if anyone else asks you that question." He did not want me to overstate my case—to exaggerate. One needs a critical distance in order to rationally analyze a subject. I needed to know better than to respond in such utterly subjective terms about a personal situation that has little to do with the matter at hand. I should refer instead, he implied, to some book I'd read or lecture I'd heard; something more academically substantial that would make more sense. To respond as I kept insisting was inappropriate and, frankly, embarrassing. I am putting words in his mouth, paraphrasing perhaps to his discredit. However, if this does not represent my professor's perspective, it represents the position of the academy more generally.

On the contrary, was my sincere response to a question. I threw myself passionately into my graduate work because I felt like a slave girl at home. In turn, I studied the object of my contempt—the place that seemed to hold such authority over me. The desire to discover the key to my personal liberty served as the momentum that kept me reading as I changed diapers, driving as my husband's career took me farther and farther away from my school, reading as I gave birth to my second child, persisting when my computer crashed and died, writing with pen and paper, buying books when I no longer had access to a decent library, working when it seemed no one on my committee expected me to, reading as I nursed, potty trained, rocked babies to sleep, begging for access to the resources I did not have—just so I could finish this work—so that now, years later I can point at a few hundred pages of type and say, "Now I get it!" Where I felt imprisoned at home, writing about home fostered a sense of liberty.

Yet, I am aware that my response, even now, is inappropriate. It is, as Freud suggests, unheimlich—*something that ought to be kept secret and private which has come to light.* In the black vernacular we might call such a response "ghetto." I don't want to challenge the designation because it identifies the tensions I have with the academy. Clearly, I often find *myself at odds with the academy—both ghetto and ghettoized. But it has to be so because the very structures that teach me how to speak simultaneously conceal the intent to keep me silenced. If I compromise my answer as to why I study home surely home and all the very real obstacles I face there will overtake me and limit if not obliterate my chances to participate in the academy in any meaningful way.*

I have answered the question as faithfully as any dedicated scholar would through both my personal narrative and my academic production. And in answering, I challenge the academy with a question of my own: Can you accommodate me?

As a student, Violet struggled to produce the kind of work we demanded of her. I first encountered Violet as a student in one of my classes during her junior year. However, I had the opportunity to get to know her better in our capstone course, Senior Thesis. At that time, I had the privilege of working directly with every graduating senior in the department. Senior Thesis is a two-semester course that requires students to create a sustained argument using a sophisticated critical framework. Much of the teaching in a course like this is done on an individual basis, outside the classroom. Generally, supervising senior theses is demanding work. For students like Violet, who had been unsuccessful on her first attempt, it was more so. In addition to the rigorous coursework, students who fail often carry shattered egos into the next attempt that further complicate the writing process.

On one occasion, I was struggling as I sat opposite Violet in my office. I had just read the most recent draft of her senior thesis on Octavia Butler's Kindred. *The argument was finally clear but her supporting evidence seemed random. So I asked her a very pointed question about how a particular aspect of her argument related to the novel. Violet replied:*

> *Women bear their scars on their bodies. My grandmother has scars all over her legs from the time my granddaddy pushed her down the stairs. That was the last time he was home. I'm not saying that it's only true that*

> *women carry scars because my granddaddy has a scar from the time when my grandmamma stabbed him in the back...*

I could not have been more confused by her response. I started to interrupt but I resisted that compulsion. I decided instead to follow her, if I could, to see where she was leading.

Violet continued to unravel a sordid tale of a tragic past that brought me finally to a flood when her grandmother had to wade to the church on her wedding day. It was, in fact, a well-told tale that rivaled Butler's fiction for my attention—complete with characterization, conflict, and resolution. I had become captivated by this personal testimony of struggle and endurance. Then my student made the connection back to the novel. The water that her grandmother wades through serves as a rank baptismal pool, like the one Dana unwittingly encounters in Kindred *on her first journey through time.*

Nothing Violet had ever written for her classes prepared me for the strength of this narrative and the insight she demonstrated in this reading. Her story, the story of her grandmother, should not be easily dismissed. Traditional teaching places little value on such readings. Suddenly, I understood something, perhaps even more tragic than her grandmother's painful life. As a first generation college student, Violet had come to the university seeking an education. We gave her one. In so doing I had, in fact, participated in a systematic assault upon her. We assaulted her.

But how could such a thing happen? I shared Paulo Freire's critique of banking knowledge in students with the expectation of a simple return. Freire maintains:

> A careful analysis of the teacher-student relationship at any level, inside or outside the school, reveals its fundamentally narrative character. This relationship involves a narrating subject (the teacher) and patient, listening objects (the student)... Education thus becomes an act of depositing, in which the students are the depositories and

> the teacher is the depositor. Instead of communicating, the teacher issues communiqués and makes deposits which the students patiently receive, memorize and repeat. (57-8)

Traditionally, those students who are not able to return our deposits as we expect are deemed failures. In order to avoid this pitfall, I offered a range of texts from which I hoped students would select those which helped them to discover *their* voices. However, an unanticipated dynamic was becoming clear.

Given the choice between a range of novels including *Invisible Man* and *Kindred* Violet selected the latter. She struggled to write a literary analysis apart from the language of her personal narrative because we told her to make a distinction between "academic" and "private" discourses that the novel itself discourages. Violet's personal narrative is compelling. Graphic experience with pain makes her acutely aware of the body and her reading of *Kindred* is filtered through this history of bodily experience. Sometimes the body is simply too present to be ignored. It is then, in moments when the body is aroused that it refuses to be repressed. Instead it imposes itself upon our discourse and demands attention.

Not all texts work to evoke this kind of bodily response. Ralph Ellison's *Invisible Man*, for example, is masterful in its ability to erase the body even as it operates under the sign of race. Perhaps, it may be the sign of race that encourages Ellison to reinforce the perception of a mind/body split. In his zealousness to gain full rights as an American, Ellison erases the body itself. He represents his protagonist as an intelligence speaking on the lower frequencies, a disembodied mind which is able to live more fully absent of body. Ellison's distinction in this novel between the mind and the body proves disorienting for some students.

In contrast, texts like *Kindred* draw attention to the body by emphasizing the particular impact of race and gender. Dana, the African American protagonist, travels through time with her husband, Kevin who happens to be white, to the antebellum South. She is more radically marked by the time spent in the past than her husband. Kevin experiences mental distress. However, Dana is marked in her body as well as her mind. She loses her arm on her last journey through time. Time, place, race, and gender determine the price of experience and such tolls are not assessed objectively nor collected equally. The novel is clear. Yet, we are not adequately prepared to deal with our students when they respond viscerally to the text.

As Laura Harris asserts, "Transformation requires new strategic approaches" (379). Changing the texts will not alter the fundamental relationship some students have with the academy. Harris also says, "Often, mainstream and academic efforts to reform institutions reinforce systems that do violence to marginalized subjectivities, rendering these potential revolutionaries complicit in silencing radical difference and subversion" (379). In order to transform this dynamic we must look for a "radical difference" to emerge in response to our moves toward inclusiveness. We must be willing to share the risk involved with expanding the borders of the academy instead of displacing that risk onto new arrivals like Violet. We must all be "at risk." *Instead I had left her stranded. Violet read Butler through the frame of her familial past and as an agent of the institution I was willing to cut through the meat of her experiences with a critique sharp enough to sever bone. Like Dana who returns permanently disfigured after her confrontations with the past, I feared Violet had been maimed by her encounters with us.*

After she graduated, I went to visit Violet at her father's house. I remember a lot about our talks, in the classroom and the office, but the thing that impressed itself most firmly upon my mind is the expression she used in our conversation at her father's home. Violet punctuated our discussion about how she'd been spending her time in the two years since her graduation with the refrain, "This is not my life." I restrained myself from asking: Whose life is it? How did you end up with this life? Where is yours?

She kept repeating the refrain as she told me her story, as if the denial alone could shame the thief into admitting his fraud and exchanging this counterfeit life for the one that really belonged to her. I understood her desire to distance herself from this life, which is far too disappointing to claim. It is like Wally, the schizophrenic basketball recruiter in John Edgar Wideman's Reuben. *He fractures into distinct personalities after being torn between two worlds—the university and his hometown. Beyond the hurt he feels has been done to him, Wally is concerned about what he is doing to the boys he recruits. Wally sees himself through the eyes of this other self, "He will split the kid down the middle, from his guzzle to his zorch. Leave some, take some back to the university. Sever this boy and release a ghost that will spend its days floating back and forth between two places, two bodies, never able to call either one home" (107). His transition from the position of student to a member of the faculty does not mitigate Wally's detachment and isolation within the university. Instead, his alienation leads to homicidal rage. The main difference between Wally and Violet is the fact that the only life at risk is hers.*

Of course, Violet is a pseudonym I use to protect her privacy. I named her Violet after a character in Toni Morrison's novel Jazz. *If the African American in W. E. B. Du Bois's terms "ever feels his twoness" then Violet (in* Jazz *and my former student) is torn apart enough to step outside and look back on herself. As she asserted from this exterior vantage, this surely was not her life. Who is more qualified to judge than she whether this is the life she should claim? Violet was trying to decide where the mistake had been made that landed her smack down in the middle of someone else's pitiful existence. And I am deeply moved because I had been her professor.*

I am implicated in Violet's frustrations. As a student working toward my bachelor's degree, I was also naïve enough to believe that getting an education meant gaining liberty. It doesn't. Education is a process of learning skills or obtaining knowledge. Liberty is the ability to act and speak according to one's own beliefs. More often than not, education has very little to do with liberty. Within the system of American democracy, however, education masks itself as freedom. The system of public education and the promise that "no child will be left behind" draw education into the arena of public policy. Politics obscure the supposedly free exchange of ideas. Freedom is rhetorical; and exchange is permitted among those using like currency. Education, then, as the ability to participate in the free exchange of ideas, is not given to all students equally. Race, gender, and class continue to complicate the academic topography.

I actively participate in an enormous institution that peddles education as a short train ride to success. Violet has every right to be confused, given her difficult struggle to not only pay for the ticket but to stay on the train. For her, earning a degree had been more like a ride through the dismal swamp on the underground railroad than the luxury and comfort of the continental express. Five years after entering the university, Violet graduated from college with her bachelor's degree in English with hopes of becoming a teacher. Now she lives with her father and scrapes out a living by hassling people about past due bills.

The last time I saw Violet I was stopped at a red light. I had been trapped on a single lane road behind a car driving at a speed I found painfully slow. I was impatiently waiting for the road to open up. The car signaled for a left turn and I would have rushed pass in the right lane without noticing her except that I got caught by the light. The weather was warm and the sky was dotted with puffy white clouds so I had my window down. Someone called me and I turned to see Violet. A smile masked the shame that immediately replaced my earlier frustration. "Violet! How have you been?"

"Fine," she paused and then added, "I'm pregnant." I have never known the appropriate response to offer a young, single woman who tells me she's expecting a child—especially while sitting in separate cars at a stop light.

"Congratulations." After a moment I asked, "Are you happy?" Violet shrugged. "Stop by the campus sometime so we can talk." She said she would but I didn't believe her. The light turned and I was free to rush off now but Violet had to yield to on-coming traffic before she would be able to make her left turn.

Baba

> Then came the daughters of Zelophehad saying: "Our father died in the wilderness... Give us a possession among our father's brothers."

—Numbers 27: 2 & 4

> This is what the Lord commands concerning the daughters of Zelophehad, saying, "let them marry whom they think best, but they may marry only within the family of their father's tribe... And every daughter who possesses an inheritance... shall be wife of one of the family"

—Numbers 36: 6

Derrida (2004) a documentary produced by Kirby Dick and Amy Ziering Kofman captures one of the world's great thinkers on film. In 1966, the French theorist Jacques Derrida shook the establishment with a paper he presented at a conference at Johns Hopkins University called "Structure, Sign, and Play in the Discourse of the Human Sciences." In this paper, Derrida revolutionized the way we interpret the meaning of language. Truth, he argued, is relative; operating within a system of ever evolving meaning based on any given perspective. Derrida ushered in the period now known as Deconstruction.

The film is interesting in its ability to call attention to itself as artifact, emphasizing the artificiality of the persona represented. Derrida is a profound thinker whose work, despite his protests, easily falls into the classical tradition of philosophy. Yet, in turning the camera on the most mundane aspects of his life so that the viewer can watch him butter his toast, the documentary transgresses the boundaries imposed by traditional academics which has moved out of the symposium and into the university. The narrator reads passages of his writing while we watch him get a haircut. Facts about his childhood are recounted as he walks along the street. We are permitted into the bedroom as he decides which jacket to wear. The viewer enters the private realm of the philosopher's home and family.

This documentary captures a rare relatively unguarded glimpse into the life of a renowned theorist. Generally, the private lives of philosophers like Heidegger, Hegel, or Kant are guarded. Derrida himself is bothered by the fact that in their work these authors present themselves as asexual, shielding the most personal aspects of their lives. While Derrida is not necessarily forthright about his own love life, he acknowledges at least its significance which, he claims, is apparent in his work. As a young scholar, Derrida tried to exercise control over his image, withholding author photos on his books, refusing to grant interviews. As he matured he became less concerned with such things, recognizing that he could not fully control how his image might be read. This film is a departure from Derrida's early perspective. Nevertheless, even after inviting us into his personal space, important aspects remain consistent with the classical tradition.

The origins of Derrida, the theorist, remain enigmatic. Interviews with family members reinforce this perspective by showing their confusion about how he becomes such a great thinker. No one in his family of birth showed such intellectual promise. In effect, his mother remains a mystery. Ultimately, the critical apparatus denies the philosopher his mother. And Derrida cannot account for his birth either. He struggles to answer a question posed to him by the interviewer about which philosopher he would have liked to have been his mother:

> My mother couldn't be a philosopher... Because the figure of the philosopher is, for me, always a masculine figure. This is one of the reasons I undertook the deconstruction of philosophy. All the deconstruction of phallogocentrism is the

deconstruction of what one calls philosophy which since its inception has always been linked to the paternal figure. So the philosopher that would be my mother would be a post-deconstructive philosopher, that is, myself or my son. My mother as a philosopher would be my granddaughter, for example. An inheritor. A woman philosopher who would reaffirm the deconstruction. And consequently, would be a woman who thinks. Not a philosopher... A thinking mother—it's what I both love and try to give birth to.

One only needs to examine the tradition to confirm the truth of his initial statement; Derrida's mother cannot be a philosopher. The latter statement, however, is profound—"A thinking mother—it's what I both love and try to give birth to." Wow! In the whole of human history has there never been a mother who thought? Not a woman who carried a philosopher in her womb? Is "love" a euphemism for sex? In trying to give birth is he not merely usurping the position of the mother? How does a man "love" and "give birth" without being a woman? Isn't there a problem of the chicken and the egg—loving even before she is born? And another problem: the idea of loving that which he births recalls Baker's "royal lineage."

Of course, Derrida is right in one sense. Philosophy is created in the platonic tradition where men replicate themselves. By sublimating the role of women in the process of academic reproduction, women are denied an inheritance. In Derrida's language, the thinking mother must be an inheritor needless to say, through the paternal line. On the other hand, Derrida's perspective is still monological. His statement represents a kind of reproductive arrogance that suggests that a thinking man can first love a woman (who he claims has never existed) then give birth to her. Women must wait to be fathered in order to become a mother within the academic tradition. This kind of solipsism has characterized theoretical practice since the beginning of the academy.

The platonic tradition which continually reinscribes the European father is countered, for black women, by a tradition embodied by the African mother who passes on cultural knowledge. African women bore the stories that taught subsequent generations the myths and values of their heritage. Myths are a conduit for understanding. The African mother preserved the seeds of culture through her vernacular practices. Beyond the arduous journey across the ocean, they germinated and took root in the new land. These are the seeds that Richard Wright identifies in "Blues, spirituals, and folk tales recounted from mouth to mouth," brought over by the African mother that served as the original "channels through which the racial wisdom flowed" (40). This mother, who is now as mythic as the stories she tells, is the source of the African American woman's narrative voice.

While in recent decades scholars have established links, oral African traditions have long been set in contradistinction to European academic practices. In terms consistent with the

European philosophical tradition, Derrida expressly claims to be unable to utilize narrative to convey meaning. Instead, he adopts the language of theory. In denying that he has access to a narrative voice, he reifies the implied break between these rhetorical practices. Conversely, black women have had an uneasy relationship with theory. Barbara Christian writes "But What Do We Think We're Doing Anyway: The State of Black Feminist Criticism(s) or My Version of a Little Bit of History" "without using the self-consciously academic word *theory*" (59). Christian's reticence to rely on the overt use of theory is characteristic of black women in general at the time. Yet the alienation black women seem to feel in regards to theory does not extend to other linguistic exercises. According to Karla Holloway, "possession of the word is a cultural and gendered legacy" of black women. In an odd way these opposing outlooks collude to reinforce the perception that theory is not a "natural" expression for black women.

In *Moorings and Metaphors: Figures of Culture and Gender in Black Women's Literature,* Holloway states:

> For black women, telling is an activity complicated by a history that in addition to being dominated by a masculine ethic is told in terms that support this ethic. Perhaps it is this reason that makes the tale a black woman writer tells, just in its being voiced, reflect an urge towards a metaphysical definition of one's self... Similarly, a critical theory that acknowledges the roles of culture and gender must acknowledge that its thesis is ironically framed by the invisibility of women's writing in traditional theories of literature. Traditional criticisms often work to disable the female and cultural voice rather than to reveal the distinct articulation of those voices. (32-33)

Women's stories are circumscribed by a larger social and cultural frame that dictates how these narratives will be perceived. She is bothered by the loss of the text in the shuffle for inclusion in the company of critical readers, but authority within the academy is granted to the canon makers—not to those who write fiction but to those who write about fiction. Nevertheless, many still reject theory as elitist and esoteric on the grounds that it appears irrelevant to the practical concerns of black women. It seems to move critical discussion away from the fiction so many struggled to produce. An "authentic" black woman's voice could only be represented in fiction, so it would seem.

Since my girlhood, I have told stories that suggest for me the mythical African mother implied by so much of African American literature and criticism. Even as similar stories enter the academy through black women writers, they are circumscribed by a paternalism that minimizes their value. Consider, for example, the response many contemporaries had to the work of anthropologist and author Zora Neale Hurston. Alain Locke and Richard Wright were openly hostile to Hurston's fiction. Huston used folklore in the way that Karla Holloway describes others use myth. Although a few critics like Benjamin

Brawley wrote in defense of Hurston's use of folklore his enthusiasm is undermined by an underlying assumption that folklore is produced by the simple-minded. He describes Hurston as "taking a bright story wherever it may be found, she passes it on, leaving to others the duty and the pleasure of philosophizing" (qtd. in McDowell foreword xxi). Here, as elsewhere, we see the oral African tradition set in opposition to the philosophical European tradition. The oral tradition is seen as primitive and effeminized while the academic practice is viewed as refined and masculine.

  The apparent opposition of theory and myth presents them as "pure" rhetorical practices embodied on the one hand by the European father and on the other by the African mother. While theory provides the structure of the academy, myth serves as an interpretive framework for the masses. For Holloway myth is the cultural link between African and African American women's fiction. African American women also cite as rhetorical inheritance that text to which the African mother claims as a site for originating meaning. The problem is that the oral narrative that is supposed to capture the voice of the black woman is circumscribed by the authority of the male tradition.

Nigerian author Chinua Achebe affirms this perspective in his novel *Things Fall Apart*. This novel is about personal tragedy at the time of colonial imposition in West Africa. The protagonist, Okonkwo tells stories to his sons, but unlike the stories shared by his wives, which foster a sense of order through shared understanding, his tales are violent. His son, Nwoye, reflects on the differences between the storytellers:

> Nwoye knew that it was right to be masculine and to be violent, but somehow he still preferred the stories that his mother used to tell, and which she no doubt still told to her younger children —stories of the tortoise and his wily ways, and of the bird eneke-nti-oba who challenged the whole world to a wrestling contest and was finally thrown by the cat. He remembered the

story she often told of the quarrel between Earth and Sky long ago, and how Sky withheld rain for seven years, until crops withered and the dead could not be buried because the hoes broke on the stony Earth. At last Vulture was sent to plead with Sky, and to soften his heart with a song of the suffering of the sons of men. Whenever Nwoye's mother sang this song he felt carried away to the distant scene in the sky where Vulture, Earth's emissary, sang for mercy. At last Sky was moved to pity, and he gave to Vulture rain wrapped in leaves of coco-yam. But as he flew home his long talon pierced the leaves and the rain fell as it had never fallen before. And so heavily did it rain on Vulture that he did not return to deliver his message but flew to a distant land, from where he had espied a fire. And

> when he got there he found it was a man making a sacrifice. He warmed himself in the fire and ate the entrails.
>
> That was the kind of story that Nwoye loved. But he now knew that they were for foolish women and children, and he knew that his father wanted him to be a man. (Achebe 53-54)

In the tradition Achebe describes, there are clear narrative distinctions between the rhetorical practices of men and women. As in ancient Greek culture, men are more warlike and invested in rule of the people. Women's work and concerns are trivialized by the larger male community. They are limited to caring for the needs of the family. In the private space allotted for child rearing, the African mother lays claim to mythology. These texts are her inheritance.

For Holloway, myth provides the basis for a "(re)membrance" that overcomes the failures of traditional literary theory which suppresses the black female presence as a "(re)generative source." Myth is an attempt to explore origins and the African mother is a sign that evokes both the past and the future. Unlike the European father, the mother does not appear divorced from her counterpart. Instead she speaks within the context of the father's authority. Although the mother's narratives can tap into myth as a source of memory and regeneration, in Achebe's novel as elsewhere, we hear the mother's tale not from her lips but through the reflections of a man. Her son nostalgically "(re)members" her stories even as he moves away from them. He validates her, but on his terms. *I imagine a place where a black woman can tell her story outside of the enclosed space of the hut. Her audience is broader than children and other women who look a lot like reflections of herself. Men cook and eat. Women clean and share stories of how things came to be as they are. Words are like bricks stacked in rows until there is no more distance and they begin to rise from the ground. Each telling begins a new room that others fill with treasures as they come and go. Laughter sits with his feet bare beside Grief. The people here are fruitful and multiply.*

Theory appears to be the language of the academy and myth, as Holloway observes, is infused in the writings of black women. However, the rhetorical divide that Derrida cites between theory and narrative is as mythical as any story told by mothers to their children. Theory and myth are interdependent. Take, for example, the story of Jezebel. For many young African American women professors it is the sexualized persona, Jezebel, who guards the gates of this profession. As historian Earl Lewis asserts about the African American female identity that emerges after the Civil War, "Indeed, the nation had crafted a tripartite image of black women as either Mammy, Jezebel, or Sapphire—subservient and asexual, licentious and extraordinarily sexual, or manly and castrating, respectively" (777). What's a girl to do? The archetypal mammy can be readily adapted to the environment of the university because with no desire of her own, she adapts her service wholesale to meet the needs of the university. In contrast, Sapphire wields personal ambition like a sword to emasculate within the institution in an effort to establish a new power structure with herself at center.

Between these poles stands Jezebel whose motives for doing anything are always in question. The dyad between the "wholesome" and the "loose" woman is exemplified by the figure of Jezebel. The historical woman of the Old Testament whose name in Hebrew means "chaste" becomes the archetypal "false teacher" by the time "Jezebel" is translated into the New Testament Greek.

The historical woman was a Phoenician princess, who reigned as queen of Israel during the ninth century B.C.E. Jezebel's marriage to Ahab, Israel's seventh king, was a calculated union between the fledgling nation and the more ancient Phoenician civilization. Ethbaal, Jezebel's father, was a priest-king who ruled the coastal cities of Tyre and Sidon (known today as Sayda and Lebanon). Trade brought this country wealth, knowledge, and power. Jezebel was a foreign woman who helped corrupt the young nation of Israel by insisting upon the preeminence of her native culture even while living in her adopted land. In the pantheon of ancient Middle Eastern gods, Baal is the god of life and fertility. Although various aspects of pagan worship had been adapted to Hebrew culture and influenced Hebrew practices since the reign of Solomon, Israel's third king, Jezebel killed the prophets of Yahweh and installed 850 prophets of Baal and Asherah. It was Jezebel's enthusiastic installation of Baal in opposition to Yahweh, the God of Israel, that made her very name anathema.

Jezebel's heresy is judged by her fate. After being anointed king by the prophet Elisha, Jehu overthrows the thrown. Upon his approach to the royal compound, Jehu directs Jezebel's servants to throw her from a palace window. Jezebel's body lands upon an offal mound and her remains are desecrated by wild dogs. This denigration of the female body mirrors the Egyptian practice of throwing adulterous women to wild dogs. Jezebel becomes the embodiment of the nation's apostasies. It seems odd that for all we can learn from her story about spiritual transgression, Jezebel becomes infamous for her association with carnal infidelity. The actual historical woman gives way to the symbolic seductress. On this symbolic plane, Jezebel gains significance as she circulates in opposition to patriarchal authority. Once disembodied, Jezebel can be *any*body who threatens phallic power. The reality is, of course, that *some* bodies are more likely to be read as Jezebel than others.

Jezebel is a foreign woman who becomes an Israeli patrician through marriage to the king. Nevertheless, Jezebel displays contempt for the customs of her adopted land. Her sophistication and education do not serve her in this new nation because they read as threatening and different. In a contemporary academic frame, Jezebel is the dark other who is wedded to the academy by her position as professor but despite the legitimacy of her appointment, continues to be viewed as a foreign presence. By refusing to conform to the prevailing norms, this academic Jezebel threatens to corrupt the integrity of the institution. The institution responds by co-opting her body.

The academy claims to serve minds without regard for the body. Conversely, Jezebel is perceived as using the mind in order to serve the body. Academe needs a persona like Jezebel in order to make the illusion of intellectual disembodiment appear plausible. The academy can in Sir Philip Sidney's words, "lift up the mind from the dungeon of the body" by imprisoning Jezebel. Like the Hottentot Venus, Jezebel is reduced to her body but she refuses to accept the designation and so she must be killed. Jezebel appears as the body that threatens to overwhelm the mind. By containing Jezebel as a libidinous presence within the body of a woman, the (male) mind is liberated to transcend bodily constraints. However, the (male) body does not disappear as we "lift up the mind;" it is simply displaced. Since we cannot ever really get rid of the body, we are encouraged to ignore it. Jezebel is assigned the responsibility for corrupting the morals of men— men, we are to assume, who would otherwise be purely intellectual. Working within the institution, then, Jezebel reinforces the illusion of male intellectual superiority by functioning as a repository for amoral sexual desire. She is the unredemptive figure whose every yearning leads others astray. If, perchance, intellectual stimulation leads to physical titillation, then the desire originated with Jezebel rather than elsewhere.

Once the sexualized persona of Jezebel is projected onto the African American woman, she disrupts academic production. The designation of Jezebel morally and ethically discredits the black woman and effectively keeps African American women professors intellectually impoverished. It is difficult for these women to find and to retain mentors. They are not invited to participate in activities that might introduce them to influential professional circles. Positive traits like creativity, motivation, and commitment in the profession are interpreted through her identification with Jezebel as manipulation, ambition, and control. One must always wonder with whom she slept to secure advancement. Of course, if you are the one who promoted her then we already know, don't we? Those who bear the mark of Jezebel are shamed into silence. This kind of denigration promotes the view of the African American woman as alien to the legitimate work of the academy. Her academic accomplishments are undermined by her apparent lack of moral refinement. Ultimately, Jezebel is a myth that my father tells. He enters into the enclosed space of the dwelling to recount a tale about women. The woman's voice is lost under the weight of his retelling. The myth of

Jezebel supplants the actual historical woman and is used in theory to justify male dominance.

Theory emerges as the "master" narrative in contrast to mythology because of the evolution of the academy. This "master" narrative is authoritative. Myth is subordinated in order to support this illusion. Although theory and myth perform two interdependent interpretive functions they are assigned different values. Moreover, they are imbued with "essential" qualities that are associated with a particular type of people, distinctions usually determined along race, gender, and class lines. The scholarly apparatus is prepared to accept the African mother as storyteller but is unwilling to recognize her as heir within a European patriarchal philosophical tradition.

This juxtaposition of narrative functions, in this case of theory and myth (which again might be identified as the "father's law" and the "daughter's story") leads to the type of symbolic overreaching we discussed previously in relationship to Houston Baker's *Blues, Ideology*. Baker, however, is riding his mule along a well-worn path. In addition to the voices of Marx,

Freud, Derrida, and Du Bois, we can recognize the influence of French philosopher Jacques Lacan in Baker's work. According to Lacan, the phallus is the "signifier intended to designate as a whole the effects of signified, in that the signifier conditions them by its presence as signifier" (285). In this line of reasoning, the phallus alone has enough signifying power to stand for all other signs. Lacan assigns undue significance to the male identified term "phallus" and in so doing perpetuates its grotesque privilege. In *The Daughter's Seduction: Feminism and Psychoanalysis* Gallop critiques this perceived privilege stating, "It is glaringly disproportionate for one particular signifier to 'designate' the whole of the effects of signification. By what right does this part, this portion signify, represent the whole?" (20). The phallus is but one of an infinite choice of symbols although it circulates as the preeminent symbol of power. In his reading of the Trueblood episode, Baker reinforces the symbolic dominance the phallus holds within the African American literary tradition. He validates the discursive tyranny of the penis (turned phallus) by justifying the daughter's rape with the authority of the father's law.

In "Mama's Baby, Papa's Maybe: An American Grammar Book," Spillers identifies some of the complications associated with the father's law when read within the cultural context of slavery. In order to maintain white, male authority and black subjugation, the law insisted that slaves "follow the condition of the mother" thereby ensuring that white men would not be expected to serve as "fathers" to the offspring sired among the slave population. Furthermore, the law had the practical impact of sanctioning violence as a means of securing black women's sexual subjugation. For these reasons, the already questionable identity of the father is further obscured by the dynamics of race. Thus the symbolic import of the quest to identify the father suggested by the law is intensified within the African American community. Elsewhere Spillers writes:

> Among African-Americans in the midst of violent historic intervention that, for all intents and purposes, has banished the

> father, if not in fact murdered him, the Father's law embodies still the guilt that hovers: one feels called on to "explain," make excuses, for his "absence." But the African-American-Father-Gone is the partial invention of sociologists.... ("Permanent Obliquity" 127)

The perverse legacy of slavery disallows in ways peculiar to this population the notion of a patriarch. As a result, the black patriarch becomes hyperbolic precisely because he has never existed. In place of the father we imagine a loss so great that the magnitude of this injustice surpasses all other wrongs.

We can see this anxiety expressed in Michael Awkward's memoir, *Scenes of Instruction.* Awkward ends his introduction, "Awkward Silences," with: "The following narrative is not the story of my name, but it may explain why I loved my mother enough to keep it" (xvii). Having no overt connection to the narrative that follows, Awkward begins by addressing his familial name. The surname is a primary aspect of the father's law because it legitimates his position within the family. In this case, Awkward carries his mother's name rather than his father's. Foregrounding an explanation of his naming reveals the extent to which Awkward experiences the anxiety of loss of the father. Awkward never knew his father, being born outside of wedlock by a man who was married to another woman. Awkward is marked by his mother's name. He writes, "I remembered long, guilt-filled moments when I wished that instead of burdening me with her family name, my mother had given me the slightly threatening surname of my absent father, whom I didn't know: 'Cutler'" (xvi-xvii). He deliberately plays with language, "awkward," "burdening," "guilt," "threatening," "*her* family name," nevertheless, Awkward's name signifies more than he suggests.

Awkward writes this memoir to explain why he becomes a feminist scholar, framing his tale around his mother's influence and a series of commencement exercises. As we see him in the pages of his narrative, Awkward lies somewhere between the dichotomy represented by Baker and Gallop. If Baker perpetuates the patriarchal illusion of pure disembodied intellect, then Gallop deliberately opts for the opposite, a feminist revision of the female body as a site of physical and intellectual power—by literally and figuratively acting out of her body. (Perhaps it is worth noting that Baker's efforts have been successful in building his scholarly reputation while Gallop's have resulted in debilitating and highly publicized accusations of sexual harassment.) Although he was Baker's protégé, Awkward asserted his independence at the end of his graduate training by critiquing Baker's reading of the Trueblood episode in his dissertation. Nevertheless, his narrative reveals his inability to escape entirely the institutional mechanisms already set in place that are powerful enough to mold even resistant young men into more or less willing copies of yesterday's old boys.

Awkward titles the first chapter, "The Mother's Mark," and draws his ideas together in the last chapter, "The Mother's Breast." Awkward's mother's distinguishing mark is a wound on her upper right arm. Surgery left a noticeable scar where doctors repaired the bones Awkward's enraged father shattered by stomping on her arm. In that scar, the sins of the absent father are literally written upon the mother's body. For the young Awkward, the scar serves as "the most incontrovertible evidence of the consequences of male brutality" (182). Violent episodes like this one shape Awkward's movement away from masculinist rituals toward more feminist sensibilities embodied by his mother. Quite probably, his father's presence in his life might have prompted other forms of resistance to some of the challenges he confronts growing up in the projects of Philadelphia. However, in his absence Cutler grew to become Awkward's nemesis. "Don't be like your father," his mother cautions. Like a mythic, black patriarch, Cutler becomes larger than life and serves as the imposing shadow lurking just outside Awkward's view.

While the scar convicts the father, at the end of her life it is her breast that finally indicts the mother—indicts her alcoholism, her poverty, her detachment, her weaknesses, her failure to nourish her children. During the transport from the ambulance to a hospice deathbed, her breast is inadvertently exposed. His mother is too sick to notice or care, but Awkward notices the exposed breast with great dismay—the breast *should* be covered, especially now since it is devoid of "maternal or erotic potential" (181). Awkward had wanted to know if he had been breast-fed or given cabbage juice as a substitute for formula. The time for such questions seems irretrievable when confronted with the horror of her bare breast now. Awkward copes with his discomfort by shifting his focus to the "zipper like mark on her right arm" (182). The maternal bond that might have been forged at the breast, instead, is carved out of the arm. His mother's mark serves as Awkward's intellectual impetus and her exposed breast serves as the ground upon which he builds his scholarship. Awkward makes a rhetorical leap and adapts Sojourner Truth's famous declaration, "Ain't I a woman?" (which is punctuated by her baring of breasts) by drawing our attention to his mother's breast. In sharing his story (made concrete at the expense of his mother's body—both her permanently scarred meat and shattered bone) Awkward hopes to impress upon his readers that "black males suffer under patriarchy, too," (45).

As Awkward represents himself, he is Spiller's quintessential "mama's baby, papa's maybe." Without even the consolation of his father's name, Awkward bears his mother's "mark" in part due to her inability to provide for him a clear connection to his father. As Spillers suggests, "In effect, the African person was twice-fathered, but could not be claimed by the one and would not be claimed by the other" ("Permanent Obliquity" 129). He lacks the name that would confirm his paternity and would affirm the fact that he *knows* his father. Instead, he bears (as a burden) the name "Awkward," the sign of his mother. He muses about the origins of his maternal family name that, like most African American names, probably began during slavery as a word upon a white man's lips. But his name, even more than others, is denigrating. In his narrative, Awkward attempts to find his way out of this extended, obscene parody by navigating through a series of commencements. He graduates from elementary school, high school, college, and graduate school although due to his grief over his mother's passing he does not attend the final ceremony. His mother's legacy, Awkward maintains, is his feminist sensibility.

What troubles me, however, is how neatly Awkward fits into the tradition of African American male intellectuals. At the dawn of the twentieth century, W. E. B. Du Bois effectively establishes a model of intellectual leadership for the black academic. The first African American graduate from Harvard College, he still stands as a giant in the field of African American cultural studies. Yet as Carby notes, his model is distinctly oriented toward men

> It is the process of becoming an intellectual that Du Bois offers as an alternative route to manhood, as a way to avoid gendered and racialized subordinations, deformation, and degradation... Du Bois insists that it is his *intellectual* achievements that enable him to make a successful transition from adolescence into a socially acceptable style of manhood, and that it is the power of his intellect which gives

> him the ability to analyze the burden, the vast shadow, which stunts and deforms the growth of other black men. (Carby 34)

Awkward follows this route to manhood. His memoir suggests that, within the context of a violent, patriarchal society, he absorbs his maternal narrative so well that he becomes a feminist scholar in an effort to avoid repeating the sins of the father.

Awkward uses familial associations as a means of explaining his interest in feminist studies but he refuses to extrapolate how these ties extend outward and into the academy. He does not explore the symbolic value of these associations. Instead he seeks to shut down debate surrounding his intellectual right, as a man, to participate in feminist studies by using biological ties as justification for his institutional practice. Certainly, Awkward's participation in feminist studies is desirable because it disrupts neatly gendered divisions. Unfortunately, his participation does little to challenge the mandate of the father's law. In fact, by identifying with the position of his mother and rejecting association with his father, Awkward's narrative threatens to usurp the place of the daughter's story. Rather than transform masculine privilege, Awkward seeks to repudiate it.

I am reminded of Ike from Faulkner's *Go Down, Moses* who rejects his inheritance because he is not the rightful heir. Lucas Beauchamp cannot claim the estate because he is black so the inheritance passes to Ike who repudiates it. Ike laments his dilemma, "I cant repudiate it. It was never mine to repudiate. It was never Father's and Uncle Buddy's to bequeath me to repudiate because it was never Grandfather's to bequeath them to bequeath me to repudiate" (245-6). Ike follows the chain of inheritance back to the Indian chief it was stolen from. Regardless of his intent, the land passes to the next white, male in the family line. Ultimately, repudiation is an impotent gesture made available to well meaning men who continue to bear phallic privilege even if they refuse to wield it. Likewise, transformation of the rules of order that govern African American scholarship requires more than mere critique of male dominated society but must also evoke a praxis that challenges if not transforms existing pedagogy. A radical stance requires not only a shift in content but in form.

Awkward's memoir is monological. In this text, he positions himself as "student"—recapturing scenes of his instruction. His confessions are guarded by the twin sentinels of a full professorship and a position at an ivy-league school—the position left vacant by Houston Baker. He erects barriers that resist intrusions from outsiders who cannot speak the truth of his personal experience. Clearly, he locates himself as son within a tradition—not the eldest, not the heir, but the baby boy, closest to his mother's heart. He gleans what he can from her and then applies it to his skill at reading texts. Being so profoundly impacted by his lack (lack of a father, lack of violent tendencies, lack of masculinist presuppositions) he neglects to acknowledge his advantages. What advantages, I wonder, does he bring as offering to his students when he comes to the task of feminist pedagogy? Or is he merely seeking inclusion in an exclusive group where he might receive, as Ntozake Shange suggests at the end of *For Colored Girls,* "a laying on of [female] hands"?

Works Cited

Achebe, Chinua. *Things Fall Apart*. New York: Random House, 1994. 1959.

Adeeko, Adeleke. "Oral Poetry and Hegemony: Yoruba Oriki." *Dialectical Anthropology*. 26(2001): 181-192. University of Virginia. Springer Link. 23 October 2008.

Awkward, Michael. *Scenes of Instruction: A Memoir*. Durham, NC: Duke University Press, 1999.

Baker, Houston A., Jr. *Blues, Ideology, and Afro-American Literature: A Vernacular Theory*. Chicago: University of Chicago Press, 1984.

---. *Modernism and the Harlem Renaissance*. Chicago: University of Chicago Press, 1987.

Barber, Karen. *I Could Speak Until Tomorrow: Oriki, Women and the Past in a Yoruba Town*. Edinburgh University Press for International African Institute, 1991.

Bhabha, Homi. "Location, Intersection, Incommensurability: A Conversation with Homi Bhabha," *Emergences* 1.1(1989): 63-88.

Carby, Hazel. *Race Men*. Cambridge: Harvard University Press, 1998.

Christian, Barbara. "But What Do We Think We're Doing Anyway: The State of Black Feminist Criticism(s) or My Version of a Little Bit of History," *Changing Our Own Words: Essays on Criticism, Theory, and Writing by Black Women*. Cheryl A. Wall, ed. New Brunswick, NJ: Rutgers University Press, 1991. 58-74.

Derrida, DVD, prod. Zeitgeist Films, Kirby Dick and Amy Ziering Kofman, 2004. (85 min.).

du Cille, Ann. "'Who Reads Here!': Back Talking With Houston Baker," *Academic Search Elite*. Hampton University. William R. and Norma B. Harvey Library. 22 March 2003. *Novel: A Forum on Fiction* 26.1 (Fall 92): 97-106. <ebscohost.online>

Ellison, Ralph. *Invisible Man*. New York: Vintage, 1995. 1952.

Faulkner, William. *Go Down, Moses*. New York: Vintage, 1990. 1940.

Freire, Paulo. *Pedagogy of the Oppressed*. New York: Continuum, 1973.

Gallop, Jane. *The Daughter's Seduction: Feminism and Psychoanalysis*. Ithaca: Cornell University Press, 1982.

---. *Thinking Through the Body* New York: Columbia University Press, 1988.

Harris, Laura A. "Notes from a Welfare Queen in the Ivory Tower," *This Bridge we Call Home: Radical Visions for Transformation*. Anzaldúa, Gloria and AnaLouise Keating, eds. New York: Routledge, 2002. 372-381.

Holloway, Karla. *Moorings and Metaphors: Figures of Culture and Gender in Black Women's Literature*. New Brunswick, NJ: Rutgers University Press, 1992.

Holmes, Rachel. *The Hottentot Venus: The Life and Death of Saartjie Baartman Born 1789-Buried 2002*. London: Bloomsbury, 2007.

Homans, Margaret. "'Women of Color' Writers and Feminist Theory," *New Literary History*. 25.1 Literary History and Other Histories (Winter 1994): 73-94.

Hurston, Zora Neale. *Their Eyes Were Watching God*. New York: Harper & Row, 1939.

Lacan, Jacques. "The Agency of the Letter in the Unconscious," *Écrits: A Selection*, trans.

Alan Sheridan. London: Routledge, 2001. 1977.

Lewis, Earl. "To Turn as on a Pivot: Writing African American into a History of Overlapping Diasporas," *Jstor*. Hampton University. William R. and Norma B. Harvey Library. 12 February 2003. *The American Historical Review*. 100.3 (June 1995): 765-787. <http://links.jstor.org>

McDowell, Deborah. "Reading Family Matters," *Changing Our Own Words: Essays on Criticism, Theory, and Writing by Black Women*. Cheryl A. Wall, ed. New Brunswick, NJ: Rutgers University Press, 1991. 75-97.

---. "Lines of Descent/Dissenting Lines," Foreword. *Moses, Man of the Mountain*. By Zora Neale Hurston. New York: Harper Perennial, 1939. vii-xxvii.

Morrison, Toni. *Sula*. New York: Alfred A. Knopf, 2002. 1969.

Oyèrónké Oyéwúmí. *The Invention of Women: Making an African Sense of Western Gender Discourse*. Minneapolis: University of Minnesota Press, 1997.

Parker, Holt N. "Sappho Schoolmistress," *Re-Reading Sappho: Reception and Transmission*. Ellen Greene, ed. Berkeley: University of California Press, 1996. 16-183.

Parks, Suzan-Lori. "Possession," *The America Play and Other Stories*. New York: Theatre Communications Group, 1995. 3-5.

---. *Red Letter Plays*. New York: Theatre Communications Group, 2001.

Percy, III, William Armstrong. *Pederasty and Pedagogy in Archaic Greece*. Urbana: University of Illinois Press, 1996.

Plato. *The Symposium. Plato: Complete Works*. Ed. John M. Cooper. Indianapolis: Hackett Publishing Company, 1997. 457-505.

Shakespeare, William. *The Tempest. The Complete Works of Shakespeare, 3rd edition*. Ed. David Bevington. London: Scotts Foresman Company, 1980. 1497-1525.

Smith, Valerie. "Black Feminist Theory and the Representation of the 'Other'," *Changing Our Own Words: Essays on Criticism, Theory, and Writing by Black Women*. Cheryl A. Wall, ed. New Brunswick, NJ: Rutgers University Press, 1989. 38-57.

Spillers, Hortense. "Mama's Baby, Papa's Maybe: An American Grammar Book," *Diacritics* (summer 17.2) 1987: 65-81.

---. " 'The Permanent Obliquity of an In(pha)llibly Straight': In the Time of Daughters and the Fathers." *Changing Our Own Words: Essays on Criticism, Theory, and Writing by Black Women*. Ed. Cheryl A. Wall. New Brunswick: Rutgers University Press, 1989. 127-49.

Walker, Alice. *The Color Purple*. New York: Harcourt Brace Jovanovich, 1992. 1982.

Wideman, John Edgar. *Philadelphia Fire*. New York: Houghlin Mifflin Company, 1990. 2005.

---. *Reuben*. New York: Henry Holt & Company, 1987.

Wright, Richard. "Blueprint for Negro Writing," *Richard Wright Reader*. 1st ed. Ellen Wright and Michel Fabre, eds. New York: Harper & Row, 1978. 36-49.

CHAPTER 2

POWER

Signs of power are posted nearly everywhere dictating how, when, where, and what we are to do—shaping the content of our lives. The very notion of power suggests control and domination. Yet this aspect of power that can be so malignant is countered by a more creative element that can manifest the substance of our dreams. In this sense, power is productive and has the ability to sustain and perpetuate life. For this reason, power is at the heart of my exploration into African American women's vernacular performance. Throughout power causes distress even while it offers the potential for regeneration. This chapter is framed by a narrative that is as much about friendship among women as it is about the mythologies that shape and guide our professional lives. The challenges I confronted in the process of becoming an academic were often very personal but it seems to me they are also representative of the kinds of obstacles generally in place in our institutions. In some respects, I serve as a mere conduit like Pheoby in *Their Eyes Were Watching God,* drawn into community through the telling of a tale.

This personal narrative is told alongside an analysis of Zora Neale Hurston's life within the context of the Harlem Renaissance. While the black male intellectual was symbolically "reborn" on the North American continent in the Harlem Renaissance during the early part of the twentieth century, the black woman storyteller emerged in a more diffuse cultural awakening. Hurston's trouble was that she disrupted the configuration of Locke's New Negro by embodying his southern past. Locke did not want to get to America's industrial North by way of the Southern experience. Part of the tension reflected in the relationship between the Du Boisian philosophy from which so much of Locke's cultural perspective has derived and Booker T. Washington's perspective is Washington's overt reliance on the skill and ethics of the Southern plantation. Hurston saw herself laboring to preserve rather than transform black lifestyles, fighting desperately to hold on to her strong southern accent as well as southern ways; however, these characteristics were at odds with Locke's desire to reconfigure his relationship with the white power structure. Hurston served as a visceral reminder of that part of the past that could not be easily reduced to mythology in the Western sense of the term. And Hurston refused to relegate the South to the past. If the South was mythic, as Locke implied throughout *The New Negro*, Hurston believed it was also wholly literary. And Eatonville, specifically, was her own black place—not so much *neo*-African as it was *African* American—a distinctly black American city.

    I explore the notion of rebirth associated with Hurston's time period but I begin by considering the mythic origins of black people. Yoruba mythology provides a cultural framework that suggests ways for reading a figure like Hurston that can liberate her from the constraints established by the tradition of western philosophy. In *The Signifying Monkey* Henry

Louis Gates, Jr. views the Yoruba trickster figure Esu as the antecedent to African American literary production. However, Nigerian born Chikwenye Ogunyemi resituates Gates' reading of Esu within a broader cultural context that addresses the sexual politics working at the time of Esu's birth. By going back and reclaiming this earlier moment in Esu's narrative Ogunyemi emphasizes the difficulties in constructing a discourse across the lines of race and gender. For me, this ancient tradition disrupts the firm grasp western mythologies have had on the process of academic inquiry and validates alternative ways of engaging the text.

If Ralph Ellison hadn't already used the phrase, I'd say that this story begins a long way back—but he has. Maybe I want to say it because Ellison said it. Some stories are difficult to tell and harder to begin. Beginning might be easier if it seemed like someone had gone this way before and wound up around the neighborhood in which I hoped to be. In fact, it had begun a long way back, before I—or Ellison or even Hurston—came to be. But I can't tell that part, at least not yet. Myths take time to build...

Campus buildings-and-grounds had a habit of putting up signs so that you did not know from one moment to the next what rule you might be breaking. With just a few signs a faculty parking lot could be transformed into a lot for commuting and residential students. Entrances became exits. Do Not Enter replaced Stop signs. Routine campus byways became "Quiet Zones." No Loitering signs appeared on the wall above the steps where students hung out. Rough hewn wooden placards erected along the main road welcomed some visitors and deterred others. Later, after I returned as a member of the faculty, an electronic sign was added at the edge of campus to announce bulletins in flashing lights, telling us where we were supposed to be and when. The practice of putting up signs was infectious. Others joined in, affixing paper signs to doors prohibiting the use of mobile phones. Dress codes were posted in dorm lobbies and dining halls to restrict do-rags, bandanas, wifebeaters, daisy dukes, and other such attire. You can imagine that far more signs are posted now, issuing directives with their attendant implied threats, than when I was a student. Now, signs seem to be everywhere.

On a particularly narrow pass-way that ends with a nearly blind turn, buildings-and-grounds placed a stop sign on the end of a metal arm that leans into the street so as not to escape a driver's notice. When I was a student there was no sign on this road; it was devoid of both directive and warning. Instead, a treacherous cement block, about 4'x4'x12" rose unexpectedly from the ground on one side of the street. It served no obvious function. Without a sign, passersby relied mainly on foreknowledge when navigating the blind left turn. Two cars could not pass as safely as it might initially appear, one would have to yield way for the other or discover the impediment as unforgiving cement. Students, who were not permitted to drive on this part of the campus, treated it as a mere oddity rather than the road hazard that it was. For pedestrian traffic, the obstacle was easy to avoid so for the most part we simply walked around it as we passed through the street. But like most things, its significance varied based upon the needs of those involved in the encounter. On one day near the end of the spring term in my third year as an undergraduate, the impediment served as a platform to help my friend, Olivia lord over Professor Poppycock.

Professor Poppycock showed up at the beginning of that semester. He was an odd man and we disliked him immediately. I found him pretensions. He took great pride in the fact that he graduated from what he considered the only prestigious liberal arts college in the Old South. He had a way of starting up a conversation in French or Italian with someone else while I was still engaged in an exchange with him. He knew that for all practical purposes I was monolingual. He clucked boastfully, reassuring himself that his classical education was still relevant and strutting about as self-possessed as an aged rooster on his way to his perch at dawn. He'd learned Italian in an effort to reconnect with his father who died before he'd had a chance to repair their relationship, which was strained by his adolescence and nearly severed by his father's alcohol abuse. His father had been in love with the Italian countryside but after the great war he became disenchanted. He served in the war and never seemed to fully recover. His mother, it seemed, had also been a mystery, hidden by years of self-medicating perhaps in an effort to heal a deep-seated feeling of cultural alienation. He drew his dark, wavy hair from his mother, who was from Eritrea via Oklahoma but his stature and face (particularly his eyes) were like his father's. Through his cold steel eyes—eyes a colleague would later describe as those of a colonizer—it seemed that the rest of the English Department, students and faculty, were a gaggle of hens and so long as he was able to demonstrate through a smattering of foreign phrases and obscure literary references that he had superior training and intellect, he would continue on in like manner until a younger rooster came to relieve him of his position over his brood.

Of course, his name was not actually Poppycock. We called him that after the ridiculous expression he exclaimed when a student apparently surprised him with her opinion on Robert Frost. He was crowing about the "poet-farmer" and "farmer-poet," convoluting rather than clarifying the significance of Frost's work. A poor naive student who thought the professor's intent was to invite a healthy dialogue about the poetry dared to venture a contrasting opinion. In response to this challenge he exclaimed, "Poppycock!" He said it and then took a big breath, as if that word alone defeated all contrary reason. We waited for him to say more but he seemed utterly satisfied. Initially, we were flabbergasted that he had the nerve to use such an outdated expression in public. None of us could even recall having heard the expression before; we had read it in literature written by people who had been long dead, but never heard the word spoken except perhaps on stage. But when we had time to consider it, we decided the expression suited him fine and we began calling him Professor Poppycock.

His name was actually Dr. Abraham C. Vernon. I had come to believe that arrogance usually masked insecurity and he was extraordinarily arrogant. Because I was blinded by my own youthful haughtiness as well as given to idleness due to coursework that was not sufficiently challenging, I felt it my obligation to devote an amount of time to finding out why. After a couple of weeks of intensive study (of the professor not the literature) I decided that he wanted a woman desperately. He kept company with another odd professor, who had a fascination with snakes and the color red, with whom most people had negotiated an uneasy truce. I never took a class with her but she had been invited to speak to one of my other courses. She talked about the "man in the moon as foolishness because everyone knows that the person in the moon is a woman." She went on to speak about mythic traditions that validated her point. I didn't care to investigate further but their friendship seemed an odd pairing. He also had the peculiar look of a man who was not well fed. He was not emaciated or gaunt but he would glare sometimes, holding a glance so long that his sharp eyes nearly split open his vain imagination. I was confident, in fact, that I had figured him out completely. He wanted a woman and, I told each of my friends eagerly awaiting my conclusions, who. Olivia. Who could blame him? Olivia was beautiful, bright, conscientious but by no means a push over. Something about her always made her seem older than her years. Her body was stout and womanly, not like my thin frame that refused to hold any fat. She had the kind of hips a man could envision holding onto and she was intelligent enough to raise his kids. Perhaps the most seductive aspect of her personality was her tongue, which was known on occasion to spit fire. Having settled the matter to our satisfaction, my conclusions became the foundation for our jokes that semester. Professor Poppycock came looking for a woman he could tame and he found her in Olivia—we found no better source of amusement than imagining the antics he might resort to in his efforts to win her affection.

It was near the end of the semester before we realized the more likely reason this apparently well-qualified man needed a job mid-year. Professor Poppycock had inherited more than his father's looks. He also acquired his appetites. Professor Poppycock was an alcoholic who became depressed and binged on occasion. My father deliberately withdrew from his extended family, which was plagued by alcoholism, and passed his disdain for the company of drunks on to his children. My avoidance of people who drank too much really amounted to bigotry since I had never spent enough time around drunk people to develop my own opinion. I didn't have enough experience with alcohol even to know its immediate effects. Eventually, we'd find the professor sometimes blurry eyed and on the verge of tears reclining in his office. It's hard to be a good professor when ones own needs are great. Teaching requires so much service. On this day when Olivia and I had just reached the cement block in the narrow street, Dr. Vernon bolted out of a building. We had just left his class and we were disgusted. He was drunk and made an embarrassing effort to gain our sympathies during class by offering us the opportunity to write the final exam. Olivia sucked her teeth and walked out of class. His eyes followed her out of the room and he seemed to have forgotten what he was doing and that other students were still present. Once he regained a bit of composure he dismissed class and I caught up with Olivia. We were some distance away when Dr. Vernon swung open the door of the building.

"OOOOLIIIIVVEEE-AAAAAA!" It was like the scream Sylvester Stallone made in the movie Rocky, *calling out for his wife (only her name was Adrienne). I was startled but curiously amused. We debated whether or not she should even respond but I encouraged Olivia that perhaps it was time she spoke her mind. She felt that Dr. Vernon had been unfairly penalizing her throughout the semester for things beyond her control. She had been confused by his response to her previous attempts to express her concerns. And I agreed that her grades appeared arbitrary rather than the result of reasoned consideration. This seemed reason enough to wait for a raving drunken man to catch up to us in the street.*

Olivia seized the moment and stepped up on the cement block so that by the time Dr. Vernon reached us she was standing nearly half a foot taller than him. She was forcing him to do what he'd never done before, to look up to her. This was to be the stage for negotiations. He initiated the palaver with a question, "What have

I done to upset you Olivia?" She started with the events that had just occurred in the classroom and began to explain her frustrations. Olivia and I had been friends since my sophomore year. She helped draw me out of the funk into which I sank at the thought of leaving home for college. I went anyway but I refused to feel good about it. I might have stayed in that emotional state indefinitely if I had not encountered her ready laughter. It seemed to me easy to speak in her presence without having to offer a string of qualifiers. She understood the meaning between my words and I needed that kind of an easy friendship at that time. Olivia was also the most conscientious person I knew. She bothered to recall little victories—like the time my father took me shopping and bought just the right shoe to match the tan flower in my waist band or when I was finally able to remember the sound shifts that signaled the transition from Old to Middle English. Things that hardly mattered to anyone besides me, she celebrated. For each of these small triumphs she managed to make me feel special. Around her I felt I could say those nasty things normally too terrible to put into words* *without fear of judgment because when all was said and done she trusted that I knew how to act. And sometimes we both had the propensity to say nasty things. But not now.*

Now Olivia seasoned her academic training with a bit of fire, deliberately leaving a mark without scarring. I admired her skill and gall. That's why I trusted her enough to step in the middle of this exchange. I served as referee, mediating the two positions—deciding who had misspoken, whose argument was unreasonable, and when one of them had stepped out of bounds. I thought the negotiations were going along well until I put my foot on the stoop and Dr. Vernon put his hand on my knee.

His cloudy eyes were fixed on Olivia but he put his hand on me. The knee is not a "private" part children speak of in coded language: coo-coos or pee-pees, Chihuahuas or chuwakees. It's a knee. Yet, unlike a shoulder or a hand or even a cheek occasionally kissed by near strangers, a touch upon the knee reverberates in the flesh. The physical contact reminded me that I was a young woman standing in the street with a drunken man. The fact that he was a professor and I was a student and the three of us were negotiating for rhetorical power became a distant abstraction as I was brought bodily back into the situation. I saw the street as a safe place within the enclosed space of the campus and I believed that as long as we operated within the bounds of acceptable conversation it would remain safe. But he violated the rules of engagement long before the conversation began and I was too inexperienced to realize that a young woman is simply not safe *with a drunken man.*

Abidemi

Mo k'eran
I collect meat
—Yoruba distress call

Eran ko, a sa m' egun ni,
It's not meat but the unsalvageable bones
—traditional Yoruba reply

It turns out that our palaver was more of a distress call than any kind of serious negotiation. And, it seemed, I was the one in distress. It had not appeared that way to me initially. I thought that Olivia and I were negotiating for our rightful position within the academic dialogue, only to discover that I was an exile speaking, not in the language of the academy, but in a foreign tongue. I thought that I was safely mediating between two parties—serving as an objective observer. But all that talk seems to have dwindled to little more than idle chatter. I bought into the academic illusion that presents language as empowerment. The academy dispenses education like "meat"—protein rich brain food—available for me to gather. We gain access to that education through language. I thought that I could use language as a tool to trade in intellectual capitol, garnering for myself position and power. Dr. Vernon's hand shattered that illusion. No matter how articulate and skillful I had been, my words immediately lost their efficacy. I cried, "Mo k'eran." He replied, "Eran ko, a sa m'egun ni." Indeed I had brought the meat but all he cared about was his bone.

It seems appropriate when discussing the life and work of Zora Neale Hurston who spent her entire career and years after she had been put to pasture trying to collect the "meat" of the African American experience to open this section with this Yoruba distress call. Her work is a cry that affirms her intent and belies the true conditions under which she toiled. The reply comes back in a tone of mockery rather than assistance, turning the initial plea on its side. The dark humor matches that of one who envisions in her best known work, *Their Eyes Were Watching God*, a woman who must shoot her beloved husband before she can retire with the horizon around her shoulders. Her own life did not end so nostalgically.

Although Hurston's major works were published during the 1930s, she is unquestionably a key figure in the Harlem Renaissance generally associated with the decade preceding the Great Depression. Yet her role and her relationship to the black literati of that era is still contested. From W. E. B. Du Bois's vantage, all art was propaganda and black writers were fighting for social justice. Standing at the vanguard of the black arts movement and at the threshold of the twentieth century, Du Bois was benighted for declaring "double consciousness" as the internal struggle between "two warring ideals." With her meager resources, Hurston could ill afford such a war—wars involved enemies in a clash of power. Wagging war, even a psychological war like the one Du Bois identifies as "double consciousness," requires a sustained commitment to potentially violent confrontation. Hurston simply rejected the basic premise of Du Bois's "war" of double consciousness by refusing to see herself through the eyes of another. Instead, she meant to live and die on her own terms. This didn't mean that she wanted to live as a recluse. Hurston was an artist who was deeply interested in people. She attempted to reconcile herself to the world around her through the myth and stories of her community. While the effort necessitated her departure from her native Florida in order to become part of the dynamic social structure of the Harlem literati, she was not seeking an escape. Rather, she was searching for the tools that would help her preserve the folklore she was immersed in as a child.

Hurston was never able to live independently off the revenue generated by her writing. Eventually, with other avenues of support exhausted, Hurston returned to domestic work. Her pride kept Zora from telling those closest to her the magnitude of her need. During those last years, the poverty that had been stalking her was gaining the upper hand. Her entire life she had been fighting it. In spite of the lingering threat, Hurston became famous for her wit, charm, and tenacity, as much as her published writings. By then, however, she was old, older than most people knew, and her health was failing. Her quest to reach the horizon had been hard on her, being chased by poverty the whole way. I think she knew she could never make it. The horizon is as treacherous as the moon, drawing her out from her childhood home in Florida to meet her, while steadily backing away. The horizon and the moon must have been able to see from their privileged vantages that Zora was a poor black girl living in the Jim Crow

South. Poverty would not tire like Zora; in fact, it kept vigilant watch over her like some abusive lover afraid she'd fall in love with money. Zora never had much chance.

When Hurston died in 1960 in the St. Lucie welfare home, poverty left her buried in an unmarked grave. For someone who spent her life lobbying for the value of common black experiences, the raggedness of her homegoing seems particularly boorish. Perhaps she foresaw her own end fifteen years earlier when she approached W. E. B. Du Bois about proposing "a cemetery for the illustrious Negro dead" (Kaplan 518). She asks Du Bois to use his influence to dedicate a patch of land for a memorial to those cultural warriors who labored in the service of black people, a request consistent with the goals Hurston set throughout her life. Hurston pleaded that Du Bois as spokesperson for black America, "Let no Negro celebrity, no matter what financial condition they might be in at death, lie in inconspicuous [sic] forgetfulness" (Kaplan 519). No such memorial was ever erected. Funds were gathered belatedly for the funeral which was attended by a hundred mourners. A few days later, her papers had to be rescued from a fire set to clean up after the dead. Hurston's works went out of print and she lay buried in an unmarked grave in a town somewhere south of the place she first caught a glimpse of the horizon. Although poverty latched on to Hurston like they had some perverse arrangement, it really belonged to the nation so mired in racial and sexual politics that it hardly recognized, let alone honored, her genius.

What Zora lacked in money was more than compensated for in intellect. She saw the value of her cultural inheritance as the wealth of her generation. The stories Hurston heard on the storefront porch in Eatonville, Florida became the life-blood of her work. After making her way along a meandering path that would gain her an audience before the thrones of power in the black intellegensia, Hurston returned to her childhood home as an anthropologist and accomplished author. Despite her accomplishments, Hurston was not a product of the academy as much as she was a daughter of the black rural South. Carla Kaplan, who edits a collection of Hurston's letters, agrees that "Hurston, who in spite of her time at Barnard and Columbia, was mostly self-trained" (178). Formal education came late and ended too soon to transform her entirely. By the time she received her high school diploma, Hurston was already in her mid-twenties. For reasons that remain unclear beyond the fact that she was dependent on the charity of white men with more money and power, Hurston was not permitted to pursue her doctorate in anthropology, a degree that might have secured her academic respectability even as a black woman in the early twentieth century. "After 1935," her biographer writes, "she had relatively little interest in the formalities of the academic method" (Hemenway 212). Hurston acquired many of her values while immersed in the complex social network of Eatonville--the community to which she retreats at the end of her life. This first incorporated black town in the United States provides a rich cultural base for Hurston and offers the setting for several of her works: *Their Eyes Were Watching God, Jonah's Gourd Vine,* and *Mule Bone* among them.

Hurston's work lacked entirely the element of social protest that would come to the forefront of African American literature during the 1940s-50s, the decades following the publication of her major works. Critics like Hugh M. Gloster, published in *Negro Voices in American Fiction* (1948), were disappointed that *Their Eyes Were Watching God* and her first novel, *Jonah's Gourd Vine,* reflected Hurston's interest in "folklore and dialect [rather] than social criticism." Gloster continues, "Neglecting the racial tensions which attracted many of those with whom she associated during the Negro Renascence [sic.], she usually presents Southern folk life without shame, rancor or protest." Richard Wright's *Native Son* (1940), published just three years after *Their Eyes Were Watching God,* signaled the direction African American literature was to take during the next three decades.

Wright's harsh depiction of Chicago ghetto life for his struggling protagonist, Bigger Thomas, was an uncompromising indictment of white racism. The critical success of *Native Son* was evidence that social protest had taken center stage. Although Alain Locke was deemed the father of the Harlem Renaissance, a period of revitalization of African American art, music, theater, and literature, his efforts to promote the "beauty" of black art over social "propaganda" proved futile without adequate literary outlets. Under the leadership of Du Bois, the National Association for the Advancement of Colored People (NAACP)'s *The Crisis* suggested with its name the kind of literature it would support just as the National Urban League's *Opportunity* similarly declared its values. These publications were produced by the most powerful social organizations in the African American community and were the primary outlets for writers like Hurston. These organizations were founded to address the harsh realities of black life in America and thus race matters were central to their agendas. The opportunity to publish was a chance to confront white oppression directly and the crisis was too great to ignore. Many viewed Hurston as pandering; they aligned her work more closely with minstrel shows designed to entertain without offending white audiences with the amusements of provincial black life than with the biting social commentary needed to confront head-on a society that had replaced the lash of the whip with the strangle of the noose.

Richard Wright pejoratively implied that Hurston was a modern Phillis Wheatley. She embodied the black folk culture of her generation. Hurston was not interested in engaging the "race question." Instead, she sought to preserve the folk culture of which she was a part. Hurston's biographer explains, "Zora Hurston spent the first twenty years of her career trying to show that normality is a function of culture, that an Afro-American culture exists, and that its creators lead lives rich with ideological and esthetic significance, a fact demonstrated by their folklore" (Hemenway 332). Robert Hemenway was Hurston's first biographer. Valerie Boyd's more recent biography as well as *Speak so You Can Speak Again,* the first collection to be authorized by the Hurston family, rely heavily upon the authority of Hemenway's study. In his literary biography, he reads Hurston's writings through the context of her life. Perhaps, the most revealing exploration into the mind of the author can be found in Carla Kaplan's collection of Hurston's correspondences which capture her "life in letters." The letters Kaplan collects show how Hurston is able to gain access to the black elite by capturing the spirit of Eatonville on the page.

Hemenway paints a picture of Hurston as a brilliant and talented woman barely in control of her emotions who uses her charm(s) to entice and delight. He willingly suspends his disbelief, uncritically describing her apparently mystical connection with her patron, Charlotte Osgood Mason, and her spiritual apprenticeships with Voodu priests. Boyd's biography is similar in its acceptance of Hurston's reported visions although she manages to paint her portrait of Zora without patronizing. While Boyd's more sympathetic biography does a lot to resituate Hurston's image in the public mind, it follows decades after most of the critical damage had been done. Unfortunately, in addition to helping secure her place in academic scholarship, he also encourages us to read her as less "civilized" than her Renaissance contemporaries. She is that foreign woman whose entrance into the intellectual arena is troubled by a past veiled in secrecy. In some ways, she represents that which is unknown and unknowable, the very antithesis of scholarly work. If she were white, male and born in France three decades later, her mysterious origins might make her like Jacques Derrida, who signifies the promise of a "thinking mother" somewhere in our theoretical future. As it is, however, she was black, female, and born at the end of the nineteenth century in the Deep South; and her appeal came from her ability to elucidate connections to the primordial past. Nevertheless, like her younger European counterpart, her beginnings are enigmatic.

Many of her formative years are not reported as she literally refuses to acknowledge that she even lived them. In his biography of her Hemenway writes, "Hurston had been born in Eatonville on January 7, probably in 1901." He goes on to maintain that she fabricated dates ranging from 1898-1903 and "One family member says the year might be 1891" (13). She was not forthcoming about her personal life, which allowed others to create their own narratives about her. Hemenway implies that vanity is at the root of Hurston's reluctance to reveal her age; suggesting that the lies began "when she self-consciously entered high school at an advanced age" (13). Throughout the biography Hemenway plays the role of an understanding father as he examines the products of the exuberant, "young" Zora's life. Hemenway's paternalism may have been bolstered by Hurston's ruse, but Hurston was not a simple woman and vanity does not satisfy me as an adequate motivation for maintaining this deception for her entire life. Boyd offers a more convincing reason for initially shaving years off her age as the offer for free education to students under the age of twenty-five.

Zora's childhood was spent mainly in Eatonville where her father, John Hurston's position as local minister and mayor were buoyed by her mother, Lucy Potts. The family was torn apart when her mother died just as Hurston entered her teens. She was sent to boarding school and all but abandoned by her father a few years later. During most of the "lost decade" Zora lived from house to house. The experiences of a girlhood, especially one spent in exile, are crucial to personal development. Whoever Zora Hurston became had a lot to do with those years she chose not to recall. The middle passage of Hurston's life, that part of her journey that takes her from her childhood into womanhood, the middle years of her youth are veiled like so many other stories that recount the African American woman's experience of the nineteenth century.

In my daily life, there seems no end to idle chatter about an infinite number of meaningless occurrences, like the pass-times of a make-believe character on a television show or how the ice cream I bought from the grocery store melted on my tongue because it was made with only cream, milk, vanilla, and sugar. When I was in college my friends and I could talk for an hour about what product worked best to keep a curl from dangling in our eyes. I practiced the art of talking to anyone about any small thing. Like a bird on a line, I could chirp merrily to another perched nearby. Aimless chatter. Small and incessant. Then something happens, like a professor putting his hand on my knee and the chatter seemed to stop. It was a small gesture, like so many of the other topics that occupied my conversation but the violation it represented was large enough to boggle my brain and leave my tongue cowering behind my teeth. This was not the subject of idle chatter; it felt more like a whisper—a secret already fermenting because it would not keep.

The inclination to talk is stymied by the reluctance to impose the responsibility associated with that knowledge upon the listener. Some stories, like the one Toni Morrison tells in Beloved, are not to be "passed on." How do you tell the story of violation? And to whom? I had not been raped nor had I killed as Sethe in Beloved had done—it was just a hand on my knee but I could see myself as a lion taking his arm off with a swipe of a giant clawed paw and walking away before he had time to start bleeding. As it was, fingernails make poor substitutes for claws and I was dismayed that my words were the only weapons at my disposal. They seemed so empty beneath the weight of his hand. "You need to get your hand off of me," I said, refusing to move my leg. It was a test of wills and my resolve was my strength.

He stopped staring at Olivia long enough to feign surprise, "See how you treat me?" He moved his hand slowly. I moved my foot from the platform to the street. I had lost *track of the discussion but Olivia was still going with a head full of steam. Then Dr. Vernon broke in, "I'm about to get myself in trouble."*

"Don't," I suggested as if touching me wasn't trouble already.

"No. Go ahead. I can take whatever you have to say," Olivia was braced for criticism.

"I'm about to get myself in trouble," Dr. Vernon repeated.

"You don't want to hear what he's thinking. Trust me." I turned to Olivia, thinking I might get through to her instead. So many times in the past she listened past my words but she did not hear me now. Both of them seemed impervious to my warnings. Warnings? It was too late for warnings. My reflexes were dull and I was slow to react. The discussion had already gone south and I was feeling a growing urge to escape. I was indeed distressed.

"Go ahead. Go on and say what you're thinking," Olivia was growing increasingly agitated. Something had disrupted our line of communication and I felt a simmering need for escape.

I'd sat my book bag down just as Dr. Vernon caught up to us so I bent to pick it up. Although I was now more than ready to leave, it felt rude to walk off without some sort of indication other than my departure. My manners held, exercising their meager authority in this situation. Nevertheless, I was contemplating simply walking away when I became paralyzed by the unnaturalness of Dr. Vernon's pose. He had raised his right hand toward Olivia as if he was suddenly suffering from the delusion of being in a casting call for a Shakespearean tragedy and he was reading the part of Romeo dumbstruck by Juliet on her balcony like the morning sun. His mouth opened and he declared, "If there are any two people I'd fall in love with," I couldn't move. "It would be you," Dr. Vernon gestured toward Olivia. "And you," he turned his head to look at me. That was it. I'd heard enough. A sudden impulse put my feet in motion and despite the fact that I wasn't facing the direction I intended to go, I didn't want to waste the time it would take to turn around. I walked to the edge of the building and rounded the corner and when I supposed I was out of sight, I dropped down on the curb. I was numb again.

A moment later Olivia stopped in front of me, "Do you mind if I join you?" My chin was resting on my knees. I couldn't bother to look up.

"No."

She sat down. "You saw that coming."

"Yes. I tried to warn you."

"I didn't know that's what he wanted to say."

"Yeah," I tried to nod but the gesture was halted when my teeth met like linebackers on the gridiron against an unforgiving knee. Then it was too painful to say anything else. We sat for sometime in silence.

Hurston's autobiography, *Dust Tracks on a Road*, is notoriously unreliable. Alice Walker, perhaps Hurston's biggest champion, says that it "rings false" (91). It's full of half-truths and whole-lies that have the effect of keeping her "real" life secret even as it masquerades as autobiography. Hurston wrote the book upon the urging of her publisher who thought that the public would buy the story. Hurston remained reluctant about revealing her personal life even as she wrote, published, and promoted the book. Perhaps she believed that she found a compromise, in her approach to writing *Dust Tracks*, that would afford her the safety of a private place, some distance removed from public scrutiny, while she appeased her publishers with a story that might satisfy her readers. Whatever her reasons for writing, it was done.

For African Americans living during the turbulent period represented in the book it seemed implausible that Hurston could describe a personal history untroubled by the violence that tormented blacks elsewhere. After all, the massacres of the vital African American community of Greenwood in Tulsa, Oklahoma in 1921 and of the black community of Rosewood, Florida in 1923 (about one hundred twenty-five miles northwest of Eatonville) are graphic reminders of the precarious status of black people in America. The systematic dismantling of so many signs of black progress from the time following Reconstruction up to the Civil Rights Era makes Eatonville, as Hurston describes it, seem mythic. If an African American audience as represented by the voices of her contemporary critics were not prepared to deal with her failure to confront racism in her fiction, she lost the support of many of her most ardent advocates when she refused to acknowledge its impact on her life.

More than anything, *Dust Tracks* demonstrates Hurston's capacity for "telling lies," but it also shows us the failure of established genres to accommodate a figure like Hurston. Taken in conjunction with her other works, these stories function like a cultural repository for values and traditions that might otherwise be lost. Hurston well knew that hers was a dynamic culture, constantly adapting to a rapidly changing environment. As social pressures shifted, so too would the black response. Even without agitation from white racists in an environment like Eatonville, oral practices are always transforming. Storytellers were expected to entertain, often the same audience on a routine basis, so their tales stretched and lied as intrinsic to the effort. Lying is part of the culture Hurston studied as an anthropologist, capturing the flavor of the African American folk. If these "lies" present in her autobiography do little to reveal the specific details of Hurston's personal life, they reveal something about the general nature of her upbringing that made her distinct from her contemporaries.

Of those who became famous writers during the 1920s and 1930s, only Hurston was born and raised in the rural South. Langston Hughes was raised in the Midwest; Sterling Brown was born in Washington, D.C.; W. E. B. Du Bois was raised in Massachusetts; Chester Himes was raised in Missouri; Countee Cullen was from New York; Alain Locke from Philadelphia; Jessie Fauset grew up in New Jersey; Claude McKay was Jamaican. Arna Bontemps was born in Alexandria, Louisiana but moved with his family when he was three years old to California; only Alice Dunbar-Nelson was raised in a southern city, New Orleans. With the exception of Hurston, the Harlem literati emerged from the black working or middle class and they were not from the rural South. Migrants tended to distance themselves from their folk roots as they integrated into more cosmopolitan settings while those who remained "back home" were more likely to maintain African retentions. Perhaps, Hurston's rearing situated her closer to a more "authentic" black root.

Zora was different from her peers; something about her manner appeared unreconciled to her northern surroundings. Hemenway maintains that, "she refused to repudiate the folk origins that were such a rich part of her total identity... She abhorred pretense, and she had no desire to adopt a bourgeois respectability" (27). She had a reputation for lacking "discipline"—the word "discipline" merely a euphemism for "class." As Walker notes, "With her easy laughter and her Southern drawl, her belief in doing 'cullud' dancing authentically, Zora seemed—among these genteel 'New Negroes' of the Harlem Renaissance—*black*" (89). Despite her fame and intellectual accomplishments, Hurston remained grounded in the poorest caste of Americans. It was from here that she drew the strength of her character. As a writer, she hoped to bring her knowledge of folk culture to the attention of the masses. In her role as an anthropologist, Hurston hoped to preserve the oral practices of her generation. This was her distinct contribution to the burgeoning field of African American arts.

In 1932, Hurston chose to return to Florida. It is Florida rather than New York that she considers a place of rebirth. Hurston's vision is creative ("generative" in the language of Karla Holloway) and she adapts the terminology of the Harlem literati and resituates it within the context of the South—the place of her own birth. In a letter to her former patron, Charlotte Mason, Hurston writes, "Perhaps I shall never roll in wealth. That is not the point. If we can give *real* creative urge a push forward here, the world will see a *New Negro* and justify our efforts. That is pay" [second emphasis added] (Kaplan 277). Hurston's vision is to build Negro theatre and art dedicated to a more "authentic" source. For Hurston, that source is located in the black community of the South.

Although Hurston returns to her native Florida, in many ways she was an exile in the sense that Wole Soyinka suggests ex-*Ile*. The Noble Laureate, Soyinka lived in exile from Nigeria for many years. His experience prompted him to reflect on the meaning and condition of being in exile. In *Isara: A Voyage Around "Essay,"* he pairs the Latin prefix "ex," meaning "out" with the Yoruba "*Ile*," which means "house," to convey the sense of being "away from home." Soyinka's "ex-*Ile*" embodies the tensions associated with African people working in a Western tradition. The authority of the dead Latin tied to the local vibrancy of the Yoruba represents the fusion of disparate linguistic and cultural practices. In the essay that serves as the foreword of Hemenway's biography, Alice Walker writes that "Zora was more like an uncolonized African than she was like her contemporary American blacks" (xiii). For Hurston, of course, the Yoruba language of West Africa had already been displaced by the Southern dialect of the black American South but she had the nearly unimaginable privilege of growing up black in America under black sovereignty. Although the authority of the town's leadership is circumscribed by white supremacy, Eatonville is a black home place, replicating in content, if not in form, pre-colonial West Africa. Consequently, for Hurston already removed from the African experience by the intervention of the Middle

Passage and slavery, she is further exiled by her effort to gain access to the black literati. Eatonville, as it was with pre-colonial Africa, proves not to be a self-contained universe and when considered in relationship to the context of the Jim Crow South the institutions that grant such entree are necessarily elsewhere. The journey she must make to acquire a literate discourse acceptable to the American publishing industry makes her an exile by demanding that she leave home. Hurston's quest "to reach the horizon" draws her out of the "house" and away from home even as that home serves as the source of her strength.

Almost certainly Walker's suggestion exaggerates a romantic link, a gesture that says at least as much about Walker's desire for stronger ties between herself and West Africa as it says about the nature of the link with Hurston. Walker fulfills her need for a black female role model by assigning enormous significance to Hurston as a literary figure. Pre-colonial Africa occupies such a profound void in traditional American literary studies that its very invocation is mystical. Just calling such a place to mind requires an act rather like conjuring—having to imagine *something* out of *nothing*. I would suggest that as we examine the role Hurston plays in the tradition of American literature we must consider her in relationship to conflicting ideologies. On the one hand, the practice dominated by Western philosophy is becoming increasingly sterile as it relies on the perception of objectivity (particularly when Hurston is writing, during the period between the first and second World Wars, a time of heightened anxiety about eugenics). This tradition is opposed by a figure like Hurston who brings obvious biases to her work. But if we are willing to acknowledge that "objectivity" is merely another belief system in the company of other systems designed to create order and meaning out of the randomness of life, then we can see Hurston differently. Rather than a curiosity, like Derrida she seeks to bring order to chaos by insisting upon the value of her own cultural practices. I am not suggesting, however, that Hurston and Derrida be collapsed into the same intellectual category. I am saying that the more scientific methodologies employed by a philosopher/teacher working out of the Platonic tradition are no closer to the truth of the human experience than a *raconteusse* sharing age-old stories with children. In one tradition, knowledge is gained by displacing previous innovations with more technological advancements; in the other, wisdom is gleaned by those closest to the originary source.

For all her academic, economic, and social failings, Hurston manages to construct, at least in part, a myth of origins that counters others and establishes a place for her within a larger pantheon of beliefs. Eatonville becomes Hurston's *ile*; her aboriginal house and her place of beginnings, which she utilizes as an author. According to scholar Karla Holloway, within the African context mythology *is* literature rather than part of literature as Westerners teach. She argues that black women's writing rests upon the refusal to distinguish between myth and literature. Authors like Toni Morrison who "remember" a lost history in a novel like *Beloved* are participating in ancient cultural practices. Morrison, Hurston and others like Shirley Anne Williams, Octavia Butler, Margaret Walker, and Gayl Jones attempt to recover crucial aspects of

African American history by becoming the mythmakers of their generation. "Mythologies are the reconstructions of memory—the meta-matrix for all uses of language and the primary source of a literature that would recover a historical voice that is at once sensual, visceral, and real" (Holloway 107). For those working in this tradition, memory is a viable alternative to history; and myth, like the story Hurston tells about her birth in *Dust Tracks*, is the expressive medium.

The opening passage of *Dust Tracks* positions Hurston within a network of mythic traditions. She begins her autobiography by asserting her connection to the land and laying claim to an ancient site of memory: "Like the dead-seeming, cold rocks, I have memories within that came out of the material that went to make me. Time and place have had their say" (1). This initial statement suggests a connection with the earth, thus reasserting the familiar notion of "Mother Africa"—the continent that brought forth human kind. The connection is mystical, rather than natural, because it is beyond the capacity of natural sensory perception. The rocks that seem to be "cold" and "dead," according to scientific methodology, remember and, even more remarkably, share those memories with her as an intrinsic part of her being. Hurston constructs for herself a myth of origins to rival the tales that have been told about her. Despite the fact that the first chapter is labeled "My Birthplace," Hurston was not born in Eatonville; she was born in Alabama where her father was a sharecropper. So from the start, her memoir is fraught with inaccuracies. But we can interpret this text in the context of a complicated society that had imposed a number of lies of its own. Although her efforts are not entirely successful, I see Hurston trying to adapt mythic imagery, which might otherwise reduce her to a stereotype and to utilize myth as a means of expanding her intellectual territory. So Hurston invents an alternative to the "objective" reality of her life in the form of her writings.

Hurston rejects the fact that she is born to an impoverished Alabama landscape and exaggerates her relationship to Eatonville, laying the foundation of her own *ile*. In the way that Albert Murray suggests, South is a very old place to which Hurston asserts her intrinsic ties. The very substance of her being is the same as that of the Earth. And she goes on to maintain that the place from which she comes is black—meaningfully and substantially. She reifies this declaration by underlining the content with a complimentary black form. She uses the idiom of black folk and says, "I was born in a Negro town. I do not mean by that the black back-side of an average town" (1). The hyphen in this quotation saves for Hurston a measure of genteel respectability but she is too enmeshed in folk practices to miss the pun. Her contemporary Gertrude "Ma" Rainey sang throughout the South, playing off a similar pun. Black people have noted with some amount of amusement that bottoms have a peculiar way of being blacker than the rest of the body and given the private nature of the derriere, such an observation is, by definition, an inside joke. Invoking the bodacious blues spirit expressed by "Ma Rainey's Black Bottom," at the opening of her autobiography, Hurston decidedly turns her back to her audience (white and black). By presenting this information to the general populace, Hurston exposes her own bottom, in effect, beginning her autobiography with a mooning. She starts her tale with a gesture of defiance to a world that segregates and restricts black people. By laying claim to a black place that sought to "incorporate" itself into the American schema on equal terms, she turns her back on a racist culture.

Palava

> He shook my hand gravely, without surprise or distaste. I looked down, he was there somewhere behind the lined face and out stretched hand. "And now our palaver is finished," I said. "Good-bye."
>
> —Ralph Ellison, *Invisible Man*

Hurston's back was turned on a racist white America, but she was facing an encompassing black Africa. It was no easy task for her to find her footing when she was looking across a wide ocean for balance and support. Whatever measure of success she had in undertaking this feat was accomplished by utilizing the broad scope of myth and folklore as a lens. As an ocular in the hands of African Americans during the early part of the twentieth century, mythology had the peculiar ability to make it appear as if Africa stepped from behind the horizon and implanted itself deep in American soil. The ability to see herself as connected to Africa served an integral function in defining Hurston's professional identity. Likewise for Claude McKay

Signage identifying a room in Cape Coast Castle, a commercial fort built by Europeans in Ghana on the West African Gold Coast for trading in slaves

and others, myth is powerful enough to envision Africa as a "motherland," who can awaken at his call and labor again. Africa is personified in McKay's poem, "Exhortation" as it is in so much of the "New Negro's" artistry. The notion that Africa can be like a mother to the burgeoning class of black intellectuals is part of the mythology utilized by the Harlem literati. It is imagined, in part, to counter the mythology proffered by the establishment that vilified black people and reduced them to a servant class while reinforcing white supremacy. Traditional mythology is seamlessly integrated into the academic machinery and masked by its claim of objectivity. In contrast, this mythology is not self-effacing. This divergent mythology deliberately draws upon Africa as an alternative source for intellectual stimulation. Instead of being masked as "science" that asserts itself as indisputable "truth" supported by logic and reason, this mythology about Africa is drawn in broad, sensual strokes that emphasize a distinct racial bias.

From at least one vantage, little discernible difference separates science from mythology. After all, science held to the "truth" of racial difference for centuries, justifying in increasingly inhumane ways the myth of white superiority. If science has been sterilized and kept off limits to black people then it is reasonable for them to utilize the available apparatus to insert themselves in the academic dialogue. So we see a figure like the irascible Zora Hurston pick up a measuring tool and document the sizes of people's heads she encounters on the streets of Harlem. Langston Hughes reflected, "Almost nobody else could stop the average Harlemite on Lenox Avenue and measure his head with a strange-looking anthropological device and not get bawled out for the attempt, except Zora, who used to stop anyone whose head looked interesting, and measure it" (qt in Boyd 114). She was an anthropologist, co-opting the tools of the trade in an attempt to transform the field. But we know Hurston for her use of myth and language rather than for her measurements, the former proving to hold a greater truth than the latter. Yet, it is her ability to use the tools of the trade along with her access to the black populace as subject that gains her entree to the academic establishment. Unfortunately, neither access nor the skills associated with the trade are enough to overcome the racist and sexist practices of an institution intent on justifying its racial biases to offer Hurston an opportunity to engage in a meaningful exchange. Academic institutions placed restrictions upon Hurston until she finally walks away in frustration. Hurston never acquires the scientific veneer of a Ph.D. in anthropology, working under the auspicious Franz Boas alongside the likes of Melville Herkovitz. She turns, instead, to literature.

Writing becomes for Hurston, at least in one sense, a means of negotiating between the competing tensions of her world. She was trying to find a discursive space in which she might maneuver even as she struggled to claim a physical place as home. Hurston is a lot like the Nigerian women writers described by Chikwenye Ogunyemi in *African Wo/man Palava*. She writes, "Without literary foremothers to call her own in the genre of the novel, the novelist knows she is descended from generations of ranconteuses, who told their children folk tales, and professional folklorists, whose voices were heard not too far from their own moonlit compounds" (120). As an African American woman novelist, Hurston is also descended from this tradition of storytellers. When the academic route paved by the labor of Papa Boas, as Hurston playfully called the great anthropologist, seemed finally to have proved itself unfruitful, Hurston falls back on the lineage of her black mothers, which was far removed from the ivory towers. In the pre-colonial West African context, in the dim light of the compound women told tales that passed on traditions and values to their children. African women carried the vestiges of their culture across the ocean in the form of folktales and mythology. This is the tradition to which Hurston turned to validate her craft.

In some ways Hurston was aligned with her contemporaries who were also rediscovering ties to Africa. Black people who had been disenfranchised because of their "blackness" now sought to appropriate it as a sign of refinement, heritage, and privilege. And the petite bourgeoisie used their racial heritage as a means of garnering strength and support. The growing numbers of black migrants turned the city into a new black place wherein the descendants of Africans could dwell. Cities like Chicago, Pittsburg, Detroit, and Los Angeles were also burgeoning with the influx of Southern migrants, but Harlem remains the enduring symbol of this cultural awakening. Alain Locke wrote in *The New Negro*, "Here in Manhattan is not merely the largest Negro community in the World, but the first concentration in history of so many diverse elements of Negro life" (6). Locke's vision when taken in conjunction with the broad range of voices of that era including the clergy, conservative social clubs, musicians, visual artists, writers, and the more radical calls of black nationalists like Marcus Garvey imagines Harlem as ersatz Africa.

Nevertheless, the difference in the way that Hurston and Locke conceived of their cultural ties drew them into conflict. As a product of the South, Hurston's black home place is immersed in the distinct practices of rural life. Her cultural moorings are in the speech, dance, music, food, humor, and religion of those who scraped out a living from ruddy southern soil. When Hurston turns her back to look toward

Africa she does so first by looking at the black folk expressions of New World descendants of Africans. Locke, on the other hand, wants to throw off the accoutrements of the South as one might bury a rotting corpse. The South represents the "old Negro" born of the white regime, which by the 1920s had stagnated in the mire of racial stereotypes. "For generations" Locke writes, "the Negro has been the peasant matrix of that section of America which has most undervalued him" (15). The journey northward for Locke is merely the outward manifestation of an inner resolve on the part of the Negro to be as he once was.

The "New Negro" is in effect a *neo*-African living in a *neo*-African city. Locke's Harlem with its concentration and vast number of black people is like West Africa, Nigeria, in particular, in so much as it is unarguably a black place. Locke's introduction of the New Negro is in some ways merely a creation story that evokes ancient West African tales. According to Yoruba mythology, Nigeria is the *original* black place and the city, *Ile-Ife* is the first place where god touched ground. National census data may even appear to support this claim. At the end of the last century, nearly a quarter of the World's black population resided in Nigeria. Certainly there is a vibrant African mythology, offering a rich foundation for Nigeria's cultural heritage. Thousands of years before Charles Johnson, Wallace Thurman, Angelina Grimke, Langston Hughes, Hurston, Locke, and others converged on New York City, the Yoruba gathered on the other side of the ocean in the ancient cities of West Africa. As Robert Farris Thompson writes, "Since the Middle Ages or earlier, the ancestors of the Yoruba, the Bankongo, the Fon, and the Mande peoples have lived in commanding towns, centers of visual richness and creativity" (xiv). Yoruba mythology is a product of these urban communities. The stories that ultimately traveled across the water originated in the ancient African city.

By looking at Harlem as a place of beginnings, a place of rebirth and renewal, Locke is hoping for a fresh start in an American context, but one that is black from its onset. He was part of a larger pan-Africanist movement that sought to make explicit ties between black people globally. His goal in 1925 is to create a compelling narrative of the New Negro's imminent arrival to the modern American city. Locke establishes his vision of the New Negro by looking to a time before Europeans brought Africans to America in chains. The figure of the New Negro counters the eurocentrism of the Greco-Roman tradition out of which so much of America's urban intellectual culture has derived. Implicitly, Locke creates in this configuration a New World parallel to European and African ideals. Like Dublin and Prague Locke writes of Harlem, "It is—or promises at least to be—a race capital. That is why our comparison is taken with those nascent centers of full-expression and self-determination which are playing a creative part in the world to-day" (7). The "first fruit of the Negro Renaissance" is the young man born in the northern city without the cultural markers of the South. Instead, he is metropolitan and pan-African in his orientation. In the sense that later twentieth century African American authors "(re)member" an alternative slave history through their fiction, Locke re-envisions his relationship to the nation *vis a vis* the city of

Harlem and West Africa. The thrust of the work is northward and urban while the images reflect nostalgically upon Africa. Perhaps even more explicitly than the text itself, the iconography of the anthology suggests Locke's reliance on the mythology of West Africa. In constructing this new mythology, Locke is content to ignore the intervening years of ante- and postbellum toil, relying instead upon romantic ties to ancient West African beliefs. While I am not suggesting that Locke makes direct claims to the particulars of Yoruba cultural practices, I do maintain that these beliefs serve as subtext.

According to Yoruba mythology, in the beginning, there was no land, only water and chaos. One of the orisha, Obatala, climbed out of the sky on a chain to establish the earth. He carried with him a chameleon, a five-toed hen, and a calabash of dry soil. Once he poured the soil on the water, the hen and chameleon scattered it to make the land. Some versions of the story say that Obatala was tempted by another orisha who was jealous of his previous success. The jealous god left a container of palm wine for Obatala to discover. He tired from his work despite the fact that he had not yet completed his task and stopped to nap and refresh himself with the wine. By the time he arose to complete his assignment, which was to make human beings, he was drunk. As a result of his drunkenness, his new creations were not handled well so his wife, Oduduwa was sent to finish the job. Other versions of the tale suggest that Obatala formed human beings from the soil of the newly established earth and called the supreme god, Olodumare to breathe life into them. Some say that Obatala brought a rooster rather than a hen, and a pigeon and the chameleon came later to inspect his work. In each version, however, *Ile-Ife* is the sacred city where god and man first touched the ground.

Obatala, Oduduwa and the other orisha are members of a sophisticated pantheon of African deity who are concerned with every aspect of Yoruba life. According to tradition, these gods communicate their will through stories drawn from Odu's calabash where she holds all the stories that can ever be told. Odu serves as Ifa's attendant. Unlike Ifa, the male principal.

Odu, the female principal, conceals rather than exposes her tale. Her counterpart, Ifa, is the god of divination who presents a text through which the faithful discern their futures. The Ifa text is produced using palm nuts and a long thin board, on which marks, called "mothers," are made. However, the Ifa text originates within the private space of Odu's calabash. Like a womb, the calabash bears the word as the source of every story. As Ogunyemi asserts, "Odu, therefore, is metafiction, the mother-text par excellence. She is the primal text that contains and generates all possible texts" (28). Stories emerge from inside Odu's calabash before they are presented in Ifa's palm nuts, which are then read by the *babalawo*, the diviner. Traditionally, the *babalawo* has been a man and women have been barred from this office. Paradoxically, Odu becomes the absent female presence in the process of divination. The "mother" marks invoking her spirit even as the male participants resist embodying her physical form.

Perhaps one of the justifications for traditionally seeing the *babalawo* as a male figure is because Ifa, the god who is generally known for his role in Yoruba divination, also presides at births. Obatala is said to cause a woman to become pregnant but Ifa is given credit for forming the child in the mother's womb. Odu's significance as the one who bears the calabash, which is an extension of her womb, is diminished by the active intervention of male agents. While their interdependence insures that she will have a role in the creative process, Odu is circumscribed by male figures of power. Even as she bears the word, Odu has no authority to give body to it. The Ifa text is the antecedent "mother text," giving form to the story taking shape within Odu's enigmatic calabash. If, as Henry Louis Gates, Jr. suggests in *The Signifying Monkey* the Ifa text is the ancient source of African American literary theory, then Alain Locke and his contemporary Harlemites allude to this aspect of Yoruba mythology in their reliance on the image of Mother Africa.

In *The Signifying Monkey*, Gates writes a seminal text that explores the influence of the Yoruba tradition on literature after it moves across the ocean. He differs from Locke in that he reads the black text diachronically rather than synchronically, specifically acknowledging the influence enslavement had on the text. Like Locke, however, Gates ignores the significance of the female principal at work in the tradition. Gates uses Esu, the messenger who mediates between god and man, to build his African American literary theory. This literature, Gates argues, must be read through a critical framework that recognizes the peculiar position of the African American author who stands at a crossroads of culture. Gates makes apt use of Esu, who signifies indeterminancy and resides at the crossroads, in order to explore the ways black authors gain access to the text through repetition and revision. However, as Chikwenye Ogunyemi points out, Esu is literally born into a context of "gender trouble." On one level, this phrase borrowed from Judith Butler connotes the difficulty of defining clear gender categories, but in a more immediate sense Ogunyemi maintains that African men and women find themselves in trouble as soon as they must enter into a meaningful dialogue across biological and cultural lines. Moreover, the trouble is inherent in the discourse since the tradition is both raced and sexed from its onset.

Gates does not acknowledge the sexual politics at work in Esu's birth. Ogunyemi seeks to rectify the oversight in Gates' critical position, which ignores the significance of the female role. By reclaiming the female presence as an essential part of the divination process, Ogunyemi validates the work of the African woman writer and, by extension, the female critic engaged in the hermeneutics of the black text. Yoruba tradition asserts that Osun was the only goddess among the original pantheon who had been sent to establish the earth. She was angered by the other orisha who failed to include her in their decision making process. In response, she withdrew from them and she went off to occupy herself by braiding her hair. Osun controlled rainfall and her departure caused a famine as the land dried up from lack of rain. It did not take long before the others grew concerned about the rift as the land was devastated by the famine. The orisha brought their appeal to Osun, asking her to return. At the time of her departure she was pregnant. Osun used this fact to decide her response: if the child turned out to be male she would cooperate but if the child were female she would remain in exile. In time, Osun gave birth to Esu, a son. Honoring her word, Osun again lent her unique gifts to serve the land and Esu became the emissary who handled the communications between his mother and the other orisha.

As Ogunyemi acknowledges, even this tale lacks the convenience of ready answers to obvious questions like: By whom was Osun impregnated? And: Under what conditions? What would have happened if she had not been pregnant? Leaving aside questions for which I have no answers I would like to look instead at the relevance of sex in determining the outcome of the story. Osun declared that only a boy child could draw her back to the table to negotiate with the male orisha. A son, as opposed to a daughter, could bridge the divide that separated the female god from the others. Esu's distinct privilege as mediator is expressly formulated around his maleness so while Gates tries to make the case that Esu is both male and female his argument is undercut by Esu's prodigious phallus. Like

Legba, his parallel in Fa mythology, Esu is oversexed. Numerous myths that emphasize Legba's promiscuity and sexual prowess conclude with him operating in the threshold between the realm of gods and men. "The pun here," Gates writes, "of course, is on copula(te) and intercourse. Legba's sexuality is a sign of liminality, but also of the penetration of thresholds, the exchange between discursive universes" (27). It is Esu's sexuality in this formulation that enables him to move in and out of multiple worlds. The phallus seemingly serves as the sign of his authority.

Yet, Esu's story begins where Yoruba mythology tells us all stories begin, in the dark and mysterious space of the womb. Osun's womb bears a son who grows up to become the god of the crossroads, the place of indeterminancy and possibility. While Esu moves between realms he is denied direct access to the source symbolized by the creative power of the uterus. The female principal remains elusive. Quoting a Yoruba proverb Gates writes:

> I see the outside appearance,

> I cannot see the inside of the womb.
> If the inside were like a calabash,
> One could have opened it [and] seen everything it contains.
> It is the pleasure of the critic to open the text, even if not quite as readily as one opens a calabash (36).

Gates's desire is to open the tradition of African American literature in order to expose the tale. The storyteller is a mediator, serving to bring forth an account. Similarly, the critic works at this pivotal junction to reveal a story's hidden meaning. Nevertheless, the calabash belongs to Odu. The absence of the female voice in the passage quoted by Gates and in his application suggests a level of malevolence born of curiosity, if not jealously, and implies violence against women and their reproductive function. Thus the trouble that Ogunyemi finds occurring in the discourse and counter-discourse of African men and women is echoed on the Western shores of the Atlantic in the tradition forwarded by W. E. B. Du Bois and Alain Locke during the beginning of the twentieth century and more recently Houston

Baker and Henry Louis Gates. While Gates declares the discourse of African American men "double voiced" and Elaine Showalter and Paula Bennett maintain that white women's discourse is "double voiced and clitoral," Ogunyemi asserts, "black women's can be described as double voiced and vaginal... once we factor in their more complicated position and sociopsychological clitoridectomies... Their counter discourse is expansive. Grounded in the vernacular, it speaks to black men's and white women's discourses from a view down below" (105).

Likewise, Hurston's story emerges "from a view down below." As she tells it in *Dust Tracks*, in a rush to be born, her mother delivers Zora alone in their cabin. Her father, as he would throughout her life, proved unreliable in a pinch and her mother is left to trust goodness and chance for assistance. Hurston describes her birth as this unlikely scenario:

> Help came from where she never would have thought to look for it. A white man of many acres and things, who knew the family well, had butchered the day before.

Knowing that Papa was not at home, and that consequently there would be no fresh meat in our house, he decided to drive the five miles and bring a half of a shoat, sweet potatoes and other garden stuff along. He was there a few minutes after I was born. Seeing the front door standing open, he came on in, and hollered...

Nobody answered, but he claimed later that he heard me spreading my

lungs all over Orange County, so he shoved the door open and bolted on into the

house...

There is nothing to make you like other human beings so much as doing things for them. Therefore, the man who grannied me was back next day to see how I was coming along. Maybe it was pride in his own

> handiwork, and his resourcefulness in a pinch, that made him want to see it through. (*Dust Tracks* 20-21).

Hurston's birth is announced by a call from a white neighbor. The visit is precipitated by the fact that he knew they would not have meat in the house due to her father's absence. Having recently butchered he had enough to share. Here again are the elements of the Yoruba call which when read against her narrative situate Hurston's life within the framework of cultural distress.

By making this association, I don't intend to romanticize a connection that is tangential, at best, to Hurston's conception of the narrative. Rather, I hope to suggest that Hurston's story of her birth reconfigures the terms of the Yoruba distress call that characterizes so much of her life and work. While Hurston's father is absent from the scene, a wealthy white man attends her birth as midwife. This scene works simultaneously to effeminize him, by assigning him a place in the family as caregiver, and to reinforce his paternalism by alluding to particular aspects of the platonic tradition. If any one in this scene should call out in distress we might expect it to be Lucy, Hurston's mother, but she is silent. Instead, in this tale, the white man calls. His position as "caller" is reinforced by the double meanings suggested by the word. He both comes by to visit and hollers out to Lucy to announce his intent. In effect, it is he who cries, "*Mo k'eran;*" "I collect meat." By placing him in the position of the caller, the narrative subverts his authority within a traditional cultural framework. Hurston's text signifies on white, male privilege by placing him in distress. Remarkably, the newborn Zora answers his call. While Hurston states, "no one answered," her infant cries spur him to investigate further. At her most defenseless moment, Zora speaks, disrupting social expectations of racial and sexual stratifications which insinuate his power and her vulnerability.

This mythic story of Hurston's birth is double-voiced and vaginal in her insistence on responding from the position of authority when it is least likely that she should have either voice or authority—during her first moments of life. Furthermore, Hurston deliberately inserts her mother into the narrative by foregrounding her birth even as her father's absence is emphatically underlined. Perhaps most significantly, however, Hurston introduces a white, male "granny" who suggests the figure of the Socratic midwife adapted to the African American southern landscape. Hurston must have known that Locke identified himself as "midwife" of the Harlem school. The New Negro was a child whom Locke envisioned himself helping to bring forth. This idea sets Locke in direct alignment with the Platonic tradition.

Plato records what has become known as the maieutic method in *Theaetetus* circa 369 B.C. E. In this work we find a self-deprecating Socrates who suggests that he is little more than a "midwife" helping others to bring forth fertile ideas. Socrates asserts his rights as midwife because it was his mother's occupation. Custom required that only fertile women who had passed child-bearing age serve as midwifes. As Socrates explains, "[The Greek goddess Artemis] didn't... entrust the duties of midwifery to barren women, because nature is too weak to acquire skill where it has no experience" (*Theaetetus* 149c). Socrates moves from his mother's preoccupation with the body, as she worked with women in labor, to "watch over the labor of their souls" (150c). Men, whose bodies are capable of producing children throughout their lifetimes, should refuse to procreate in the pursuit of higher ideals. Thus the perceived shift from body to mind is reinforced by a parallel shift in orientation from female to male.

Plato uses the practices of midwifery as a metaphor for epistemology. As Socrates explains, "it is the midwives who have the power to bring on the pains, and also, if they think fit, to relieve them; they do it by the use of simple drugs, and by singing incantations. In difficult cases, too, they can bring about the birth; or, if they consider it advisable, they can promote a miscarriage" (*Theaetetus* 149d). Socrates appropriates his mother's art and uses her incantations as powerful medicine to bring forth children of the mind. These "simple drugs" and "incantations," however, suggest a more ancient tradition of root work and oral practices designed to alleviate female suffering during childbirth. Women's work. But with the shift from mother to son, from child-bearing to the sterile art of the mind, the midwife is placed in the precise position as the critic in Gates' frame of reference. Both Gates' critic and Plato's Socratic midwife sit at the opening of the text as new ideas are poised to enter the world.

In much the same way as discussed in the previous chapter, the woman is removed from the maieutic method. Consequently, the mother's physical presence and the representation of the natural birth are vital to Hurston's narrative. Although she does not speak, the black mother is bodily present. And because Zora responds on her own behalf just after her birth, her natural birth does not need to be obscured by an intellectual rebirth. In rejecting Locke as her midwife and keeping her biological father at a distance Hurston challenges conventional wisdom that establishes clear power relationships between whites and blacks, men and women, in the Jim Crow South. While she willingly acknowledges Locke's influence on her career, the "granny" of *Dust Tracks* suggests the more powerful influence of Franz Boas, a renowned anthropologist who shaped the direction of the field during the early twentieth century. Boas trained her as an anthropologist and like her "granny," looks after her as she develops until they are prematurely separated—her "granny" dies suddenly and she is not permitted to continue her education with Boas. Rather than continuing to press against an academic system that seemed intent on reinforcing white, male supremacy, Hurston abandons the field of anthropology, choosing instead to go back South to write "from a view down below."

Her writing bears the imprint of the Middle Passage, that difficult journey from the African motherland, which delivered her into the Southern American landscape. Her relative privation and racial segregation, Hurston argues paradoxically become her distinction and cultural privilege. By seeking to insert the South and her voice into the continuing discourse between men, both black and white, and white women, Hurston enters a complex series of negotiations. Unlike her contemporaries who made their way in the northern city, Hurston returned to Florida after discovering that the Julius Rosenwald Foundation had reneged on its agreement to fund her doctoral studies. By then, Hurston felt she had disappointed both Locke and her patron, Charlotte Osgood Mason. Her friendship with Langston Hughes had also deteriorated. For Hurston the tensions between herself, her black male counterparts, white women, and white men were profound. Mason who deemed herself "Godmother" to "primitive" artists like Hurston and Langston Hughes, literally controlled Hurston's productivity. Much of Hurston's anthropological research was contracted by Mason. Consequently, Hurston had to seek permission to use the research in her writing. (Despite the fact that he was a professor at Howard University, Locke was also caught up in this web of financial and social obligations as one of Godmother's beneficiaries.) As a student of Boas whose academic ambitions are frustrated by her financial insolvency, Hurston was embroiled in layers of complex social negotiations.

The magnitude of Hurston's achievement of turning the stories she heard, retold in subtle variations throughout her life, into literature has an inverse relationship to the intensity of the struggle she faced. Hurston was in trouble from the moment she started writing. Discursive practices, even more than other cultural practices, drew her into the polemics of existing social dynamics. In many ways she was like a participant in a palaver (negotiations instituted in 1735 between British colonizers and native Nigerians), forced to come to the table when more powerful interests have already decided on the terms. The palaver was never equitable. As Ogunyemi writes, "From the beginning, Africans in contact with Europeans realized that talk was hazardous, for they were literally and figuratively not speaking the same language. For the Africans, palaver soon became a metonym for calamity, and its homophone palava, as trouble or quarrel, was in place" (95). Was negotiating the academic and cultural terrain of the United States any less treacherous for Hurston than for her colonized African counterpart? She never really spoke the language of her Harlem contemporaries and it is even more difficult to know what Hurston was able to communicate across racial lines.

Most of Hurston's major works were written during the 1930s, after she leaves New York. Moving helps Hurston to renegotiate her relationship with those who have influence over her professional life. After returning to Florida Hurston writes in a letter dated January 6, 1933 to her patron Charlotte Mason, "Perhaps I shall never roll in wealth. That is not the point. If we can give real creative urge a push forward here, the world will see a New Negro and justify our efforts" (Kaplan 277). Rejecting the economic foundation that has been the basis of so many of the conditions precipitating the construction of the black identity, Hurston claims instead maternal authority over the future of black cultural production. Through her efforts, Hurston seeks to reclaim the cultural matrix that is the source of her story. Hurston imagines herself like Odu to be in possession of the meta-text. From this vantage she is naturally compelled to make manifest her creative longings. This, she believes, is the source from which the New Negro must emerge. She alone of her contemporaries could conceive of the "Renaissance" in these terms, having been born on these grounds; in turn, Hurston labored to give birth to a New Negro. In contrast to the Harlem literati (of which she is ostensibly a part)

Hurston believed that delivery should take place in the South. Despite her many failings, she never aborted her cause and she labored at it until the end of her life. Since her death Hurston has been appropriated as a maternal figure, serving as a repository for the myth and folklore that lends order and meaning to black life. Hurston has become like the African mother seen through the filter of the male narrator of Chinua Achebe's *Things Fall Apart,* only recast in the voice of African American women, telling stories of origins to the next generation.

Ex-*Ile*

> Africa! long ages sleeping, O motherland, awake!... big earth groans in travail for the strong, new world in making
>
> —Claude McKay, "Exhortation"

> KIN-SEER: Should I jump shouldijumporwhut
> US-SEER: Come home come home dont stay out too late.
> KIN-SEER: Me hollerin uhcross thuh cliffs at my Self:
> SOUL-SEER: Ssblak! Ssblak! Ssblakallblak!
>
> —Suzan-Lori Parks, *Imperceptible Mutabilities in the Third Kingdom*

Alain Locke proclaimed, and we seem to have agreed, that the work of a handful of black writers and artists who converged on Harlem during the 1920s constituted a "renaissance." Although Locke is given credit for his seminal role as "father" of the "New Negro" the idea of calling the literary and artistic movement a "renaissance" didn't originate with him. He adopted the term "Negro renaissance" from an article published in May 1925, a week after the National Urban League hosted a gala event for its publication *Opportunity*. The young sociologist E. Franklin Frazier was among the evening's honorees and an emerging talent, Langston Hughes won first place for poetry with his "The Weary Blues." The short story, "Spunk," written by another recent arrival to Harlem, Zora Hurston, was awarded second place. The following week an article appeared in New York's *Herald Tribune* suggesting that perhaps a "Negro renaissance" was underway. In his foreword to *The New Negro* written in November of that same year, Locke borrows the term as he concludes, "Justifiably then, we speak of the offerings of this book embodying these ripening forces as culled from the first fruits of the Negro Renaissance" (xxvii).

The New Negro, as it was defined by Locke and a small vanguard of artistic and social pioneers of African America, signals a shift in the cultural paradigm. These purveyors of black society and culture were not satisfied with the representations of African Americans in the mainstream. Locke's anthology was an attempt to challenge these representations and introduce an alternative. *The New Negro* was published in 1925 but most scholars identify 1917 as the year the Harlem Renaissance began in earnest. That was the year playwright, Ridgely Tornance's three one-act plays were produced by his wife, Emily Hapgood, at the Old Garden Street Theatre. In stark contrast to previous productions, these plays presented black casts performing with dignity rather than as minstrels. With this public affirmation, as David Levering Lewis suggests, the Negro is "rediscovered" by an anxious white audience. Following so soon after the Great War, the Lost Generation was disillusioned with the establishment and the new decade was just off stage clearing its throat for a prolonged roar. Perhaps, this Lost Generation saw in these neo-primitives hope for salvation. As Lewis writes:

> the Village's discovery of Harlem followed both logically and, more compellingly, psychologically, for if the factory, campus, office, and corporation were dehumanizing, stultifying, or predatory, the African American, largely excluded because of race from all of the above, was a perfect symbol of cultural innocence and regeneration. He was perceived as an integral, indispensable part

> of the hoped-for design, somehow destined to aid in the reclamation of a diseased, desiccated civilization. (xviii)

The bohemian avant-garde met the social aspirations of the black petit-bourgeoisie on the aesthetic plain of literary and artistic design. Disparate forces converged in Harlem. As Lewis asserts, "For the whites, art was the means to change society before they would accept it. For the blacks, art was the means to change society in order to be accepted into it" (xxi). During this time, a conservative figure like W. E. B. Du Bois, with his Victorian ethics, could find support and common ground among the likes of social rebel Carl Van Vechten. This common ground was found in art that expressed the beauty, vibrancy, and complexity of the nation's cultural landscape.

Although he was also a writer, Locke's own artistic work is eclipsed by his pronouncements about the coming age of a "New Negro." Locke was the first African American to become a Rhodes Scholar and study at Oxford University. Later, he became a professor of philosophy at the historically Black Howard

University in Washington, DC. Despite the fact that he was living in a largely segregated era that denied him equal access to the academic and social privileges afforded a white person with lesser intellect and experience, Locke's training as a philosopher suited him well to the European tradition of philosopher-teachers. The paradigm Locke uses to establish and justify his claims about the "New Negro" does not shift radically from the platonic form and tradition; this in turn, helps to establish him as "father" of the Harlem Renaissance. Most scholarship about Locke and this era of African American cultural production takes for granted racial equality as the basic premise of the movement. Like the renowned scholar Nathan Huggins, David Leevering Lewis writes about the Harlem Renaissance from the position of why it failed to do what Du Bois and Locke seemed to believe it would. From Huggins' and Lewis' perspectives, the Renaissance was a social movement engineered to transform the lives of African Americans. The question for me is not that of pondering its failure to actually bring forth a "New Negro" and usher in political and social change in the conditions shaping the lifestyles of the vast majority of African Americans as considered by preeminent scholars in the field like Nathan Huggins and David Levering Lewis, but why the notion of a "renaissance" is so readily adopted to this historical moment. The idea of a "renaissance" is loaded with cultural significance that ties the Harlem practitioners back to ancient Greece. The Harlem Renaissance, then, has a dual impetus. On the one hand it is a deliberate attempt to suggest a tradition that parallels the earlier European cultural awakening from the murky period of the Middle Ages. On the other hand, it can be viewed as an effort to reconnect formerly enslaved peoples with their African source.

The original "Renaissance" began in Italy during the fourteenth century and spread throughout Europe over the next two centuries. The Italian artist and architect Georgio Varasi is best known for documenting the biographies of those working in Italy during this period. The term he uses to describe this period of artistic and intellectual resurgence, "rascinimento" was translated and adopted by the French. This period of revitalization was characterized by the reclamation of the Greco-Roman tradition. "Neo-Classism" linked Europe to its roots in Ancient Greece and along with the aesthetic links, intellectual parallels were also restored to reconnect "Renaissance Men" with classical ties. The idea of the European male as the intellectual ideal is reinforced by his physical presence in and around humanist schools of thought. The philosopher-teacher re-emerges in Petrarch, Erasmus, Boccacio, Descartes, and others whose work signals a return to an "age of learning." Unfortunately, as we discussed in the previous chapter, often male privilege is wrought at the expense of women. Even the very notion of an intellectual "rebirth" has the effect of effacing the mother as the true generative source in order to introduce a second "birth"—that of the mind rather than the body.

For Alain Locke and his contemporaries, an awakening of the mind is troubled by the complexion of the body. The architects of the New Negro Movement saw a foray into arts and letters as a potential means of transforming their social situation. This perspective is entirely consistent with the tradition of writing by former slaves in the nineteenth century. Scholars like Henry Louis Gates, Houston Baker, Deborah McDowell, Arnold Rampersand, Hazel Carby, Shirley Anne Williams, and others have demonstrated the significance of literate acts in a context in which they have been outlawed for African Americans. Some, like Gates, go so far as to assert that the fugitive Frederick Douglass writes himself into humanity (172). According to this logic, the ability to produce literature is given to be the direct indication of intellectual capacity and the philosopher-teacher presents the lens through which the work is read. As a deliberate demonstration of the power of the mind, writing, then, grants authority to its agents. This is at least part of the motivation behind Locke's conception of the New Negro.

Another key component in Locke's conception of the New Negro is, of course, the black body. The body reappears in this new "renaissance," occurring in Harlem during the second decade of the twentieth century, as the black mother. Again we see the contrast drawn in terms of race and gender: Europe is father of the intellect and mother Africa suckles the child.

Images of the black woman appearing in literature written by black male Harlem Renaissance authors is generally consistent in this regard. In "'Mothers of Tomorrow': The New Negro Renaissance and the Politics of Maternal Representation" scholar Anne Stavney does an insightful exploration of images of black women throughout the era. Stavney asserts:

> With remarkable regularity, the black mother is used in male-authorized texts as a verbal symbol for primacy and rebirth. Her image signifies the past in terms of racial and geographical origins as well as the future in terms of the birth of coming generations. She represents a source of both stability and change. (543)

For Locke, Du Bois, and others who were trying to usher in a period of social transformation, the black woman embodied Africa. These scholars were undeniably black in the terms established by the nation so they sought to lay claim to this blackness by gaining access to and control over the black woman's body. For the reasons alluded to in the previous chapter, the black woman's body continued to be a site of contestation. Her vulnerability as a domestic employee in a white man's household left black men feeling impotent and emasculated. Du Bois, in particular, often railed from the pages of *The Crisis* against the tendency of white society to blame black women for their own victimization.

Du Bois and others over compensated by exaggerating the virtuousness of the black woman as wife and mother. Securing the image of the black woman seemed vital to African American intellectuals of that day because she was, as Stavney suggests, "a source of both stability and change" from whom the New Negro must be born. As the conduit connecting past and future generations of writers to Africa, the black woman is identified and constrained both inside and outside of the text by her reproductive capacity. Locke commissioned the artist Winold Reiss to produce several pieces for his anthology. In the first edition of *The New Negro*, Reiss's work appears on the cover as well as throughout the text. Stavney considers the significance of Reiss's images as well as others featured in the anthology. She writes, "She is constructed as mother, not writer; she occupies private, not public space. In short, Locke's literary text and Reiss's graphic text circulate a homologous sexual topography of geographic and vocational space: woman as birthing body, man as birthing mind" (Stavney 546-7). The point that I am trying to make here is that the body of the black woman serves as platform for the construct of the "New Negro." Moreover, the cultural context of the "Renaissance" helps to reinforce the black woman's apparent foreignness within the intellectual community. Taken together, the Negro Renaissance paints the black male intellectual as a neo-classical African American even as it reinforces the perceived distance of the black woman from intellectual work.

I knew nothing of these tensions when, as an undergraduate, my girlfriends and I thought we ruled the campus. The bliss and the arrogance of my youth managed to feed my confidence that my intellect afforded me some power in at least this arena. We went off to graduate school bolstered by these beliefs. After she graduated, Olivia took a year off before entering a doctoral program in American studies. The year she spent in transition was my senior year as an undergraduate. We kept in contact throughout our years in graduate school and during our time as junior faculty at our respective institutions. It was good to have company with whom I shared so many professional experiences. Olivia found a job at a small college in California where she could watch the sunset on the Pacific while I preferred to teach where I could see the sunrise over the Atlantic. Yet, no matter how long it had been since we'd spoken, we were able to pick right up where we left off— like we were living parallel lives on different shores. Then one day she sent an essay to me with a note that read, "Tell me if I'm crazy." About a week earlier I had received an email from her saying that she was going to send me something to read. She didn't tell me what it was about. When the package arrived, I opened it and the note and essay were inside.

The essay was a critique of her experiences as a participant in a mentorship program designed to groom graduate students and young faculty into the professorate. Despite tightening fiscal constraints, increasing teaching loads and service requirements, the age-old decree, "Publish or perish!" was heralded as loudly and emphatically as ever. One of the professors teaching in the department where Olivia did her graduate study put together a mentorship program with special emphasis on women. Olivia was selected to be part of this program. I spent so much of my time in the final stages of my degree program trying to figure out what I supposed to be doing that I longed for a program like the one Olivia participated in to offer me some guidelines and direction. Now, as I sat reading the essay Olivia sent I wasn't so sure that the program had been what Olivia had wanted or needed it to be either.

Her mentor had made a name for himself as an advocate of women and in her critique Olivia suggested that despite his good intentions many of the institutional gains were individual rather than social and that many of his professional accomplishments had come at the expense of women. Perhaps, she intimated, the biggest beneficiary of the mentoring program had been the mentor rather than the apprentice. Olivia argued that sexual politics have been ingrained in our institutions and institutions are slow to change. Implicit in her critique of institutional mentoring was the uncomfortable suggestion that sexual politics were larger than any individual, that they existed somehow in a space beyond our ability to control them.

I didn't like the essay at all. I was implicated in a vast network of behaviors that seemed to call my professional accomplishments into question and it seemed to place limits on my ability to overcome them. I didn't want to identify with her argument because it made me feel vulnerable. However, feelings ain't facts. Her logic was sound and her narrative compelling. She showed how women and men behaved in ways that were charged with professional significance. Her mentor had made a career for himself advocating for the needs of women. Despite the fact that he hadn't written but one major work and the last book was less than successful, he was being anthologized, not so much for his work, Olivia argued, as for the position he occupies. The institution needs a man like him so that it might appear to address concerns about the success (or failure) of women and minorities. By promoting him, the institution can appear to change without having to adapt any significant practices. In some ways, exposing the politics of a mentoring program of which she was such an integral part, a program heralded for its regard for women, to public discourse seemed as if Olivia had been writing on dirty laundry. But she reached beyond the program into larger academic practices. I was uncomfortable because of how I was implicated. I saw myself in her work and felt indicted for my flirtations if not for my deeds, nevertheless I could not deny the validity of her argument.

I called Olivia that evening after I had put the children to bed. "Do you plan to let him see this before you publish it?" I asked.

"I don't even know if I want to publish it. I wrote it as a kind of therapeutic exercise. A sort of ritual cleansing." Olivia paused thoughtfully, " I had to write through my

experiences and to name them for myself. And I'd like for him to know how I feel." She and I had had this conversation about the need to speak on our own terms many times in various ways and would have it again.

"I had to write my story, on my terms and I feel compelled to share it with him but I don't know if I'll do anything more than that. On one level, I think I have a responsibility to overcome my doubt and just say it aloud. Not as a whisper but in a voice someone can hear... But sometimes after I've spent time writing, l have a nightmare about an interview where someone is asking me to explain myself repeatedly. I'm unable to make myself clear and I find myself ranting like a mad woman out for revenge."

I offered my honest feedback and gave Olivia my blessing, for what it was worth. "Good work," I told her, "is rarely safe work." She received my blessing. She had decided to share the essay with her mentor. She sent it in a package of things she'd promised or owed him; when she sealed the box she knew she was tying up all the loose ends. She hoped he would receive this essay as an opportunity to engage in a *dialogue, but if she was right about his myopia surrounding his practice and involvement in institutional politics then he would not understand.*

Olivia hadn't heard anything from him in nearly a year. She and I used to chuckle about how he was ignoring her, making jokes about the invisible black woman. Or the wild black woman, whom he would accuse of stalking him on a chance encounter at a conference. There'd be police and restraining orders. Of course, the Chronicle *would get involved and take the side of the renowned scholar. Humor usually led us into our continuing discussion about our professional ambitions. Disappointed with the limitations of our degrees we talked through our frustrations, so many of them rooted in the graduate experience. "I was always afraid to talk to him," Olivia admitted. "I spoke in measured tones, careful to mute and file my words to dull any edges that might cut or offend. I felt that if I spoke up and said anything that really mattered to me I would frighten him away. I never thought he could handle but a very little bit of me." I was reminded of the palavers between the colonizers and the local inhabitants. Talk was indeed treacherous terrain. For almost a year he responded to Olivia's assertions with silence; But Like Jody in* Their Eyes Were Watching God, *"the stillness was the sleep of swords" (77).*

"Olivia, you couldn't protect him."

"Only part of me was trying to protect him. I was trying to protect myself." He seemed to hold so much power over her ability to get her degree and to establish herself within the profession. Now, however, I see the picture like a scene from Hurston's novel, only it's winter and the roles seem suddenly inverted. The season of blossoming pear trees of our girlhood on the campus yard had long since given way to other experiences. When we spoke this time I was in the midst of a winter storm. People living in the Mid-Atlantic States experience a ritual panic associated with winter precipitation. My husband had called my office earlier that afternoon to tell me I needed to come home because the roads were icy. I hurriedly gathered my things and left the building. My gas gauge had been reading empty for too long for me to

risk driving home through traffic without stopping for fuel. Unfortunately, my wallet was as empty as my tank. The closest bank was about a mile off campus, just over the bridge.

I took the bridge slowly, very slowly, and made my way to a stop at the light. At three corners of the intersection cars were involved in accidents. I sat plotting my way through and around the scene when I was rear-ended by a small pick-up truck driven by a security officer from my school. When I got out to assess the damage, I felt the bitter cold swoop of the wind around my ears. I reached for my hat, checking my reflection in the window for confirmation that it was no longer on my head. I saw my bare head, then looking past the reflection, I saw my brown knit skull cap laying in the back seat. I opened the door and put my hat back on my head. He had given me a bigger jolt than I realized. After exchanging information and driving to an ATM to discover that my bank account was overdrawn and finding the gas station OUT OF GAS I called Olivia. "Listen, you're going to have to stay on the phone with me until I get home. With the kind of day I am *having I will likely run out of gas then die of exposure before anyone discovers me."* She didn't laugh. *"Olivia, what's wrong?"*

"What? Oh, I'm sorry. I'm just preoccupied." That was the day Olivia received the email message from her former mentor. It might have been less disturbing had he reacted with outright hostility toward the essay. Instead he over reacted to something she had not been directly involved with. She told me that a couple of weeks ago a graduate from her program sent her an email message asking her if she'd be interested in speaking at her graduate school. Olivia had just published her first book and Flora, her former student, wanted to be supportive. The fact that Flora was finishing her dissertation at the school where Olivia's mentor had recently joined the faculty had appeared to be a non-issue, at least until Flora solicited his assistance in bringing Olivia to campus. While I was having my misadventures in the snow and ice, her former mentor broke his silence and sent the following email:

From:	AR@aol.com
Date:	Wed, 19 Jan 2005 15:05:55

> **Subject:** *(no subject)*
> **To:** *olivia@pacificu.edu*
>
> *I don't want to be rude, or appear angry in ways that I am not. You have the right to say whatever you wish, and I have the right to respond as I have, which is by signaling, in every possible way, that I don't want to interact with you. I would have gone on with this silent signal, which I thought you'd received, had I not gotten a message from Flora about your wanting to come here to give a talk. Not wanting to place her in a potentially uncomfortable position, I'm writing to say that that's not going to happen, if my endorsement of the idea is sought or deemed necessary. As always, I hope for the best for you, but I'm not going to participate, however minimally, anymore.*

While she read the message to me I saw her through his eyes. He imagined Olivia desperate, ambitious, and still clamoring for his fatherly approval. He thought she had been thinking of ways to manipulate him into offering his *support, which he had always parceled out sparingly to her and now withheld altogether, by using a third party. After receiving her correspondence, he'd been awaiting his chance to rebuff her. He knew that it was only a matter of time before she would return. Flora's request seemed to be just such a return. It confirmed in his mind Olivia's subordination and the influence he still held over her life. This time he would not be as gracious as he had been in the past. He was comforted by his own righteousness, which grew every time he thought of Olivia's audacity so that it began to overwhelm his senses. That is why he saw her as he did and he had not heard her "goodbye."*

The neatness with which things had been done could only have suggested closure but he had missed her cues. She'd never understood the nature of their association since, as she felt, he had not even tried to help open doors for her. Olivia had been trying to tell him this for years and was finally ready for the masquerade to end. He missed all of this. He saw only Olivia with wild eyes and a hungry expression—not the way I saw her. From my perspective, she had exposed his vulnerabilities and in so doing became a threat to his well being. Olivia had taken the tools of investigation and inquiry she had ostensibly acquired from him and turned them on him. The irony is, of course, that her dissatisfaction grew out of the fact that he seemed never to believe she could even wield these tools. Nevertheless, he intended to maintain his position of authority and he would use what power he had to defend himself. He banished Olivia from the fold for the unforgivable act of having turned the spotlight on him. So she became an exile.

*Nigerian scholar Chikwenye Ogunyemi offers yet another meaning for ex-*ile. *"Pronounced with a different tone,* ile *also means soil, land. In this context, ex-*ile *can be conceived as being out of touch with the solid ground, that is, with reality, taking leave of one's senses, as in sadness, aerial flights of fancy, frenzy" (23). Perhaps Olivia was a woman who had lost touch with the ground. I remembered the note that accompanied the essay she sent, "Tell me if I'm crazy." What was it she wanted me to say? Should I have told her to compromise her* *integrity by telling the story as he would have liked to have heard it, satisfying his ego while sacrificing her soul? Or should I have advised her that to speak is too costly and that she should shut herself up behind the chalkboard and content herself with teaching others to write? Maybe she should have told another story. Was Olivia's experience any less valid than his intent? A woman stubborn enough to tell a story that suggests she is anything other than satisfied with her assigned place has to be crazy. Olivia, the ex-ile, was not traversing wholly unfamiliar ground. I had read about other women like her; I'd seen them splayed in sundry ways. She reminded me of Zora who had to leave home in order to learn to write only to find herself embroiled in endless battles for authority—the one between her and Langston Hughes being the most infamous and next to the false accusations of child molestation, one of the most damaging to her reputation.*

After an episode at his mother's home in Cleveland, Hughes writes to Carl Van Vechten, a mutual friend, "Do you think she is crazy, Carl?" (qt. in Mule Bone *204). Perhaps Hurston had given him reason to wonder. Hurston had collaborated with Hughes to adapt her short story "Bone of Contention" into a play, and* Mule Bone *became both literally and figuratively a bone of contention. Reacting to a perceived threat to her ownership of the play as intellectual property, Hurston makes a trip to Cleveland to confront Hughes. Hughes responds by trying to assert his rights over the same play. Robert Hemenway paints the conflict as an exchange between a paranoid and manipulative Hurston and a valiant Hughes. Hughes' biographer, Arnold Rampersad, describes Hurston like a mad woman with quixotic behavior acting out of jealousy and insecurity. Rampersad writes mockingly of Hurston, "she exhibited a mental power so volatile, and cherished notions about Africa so novel for her class and race, that her inability to control herself was perhaps finally excusable" (qt. in* Mule Bone *206). Yet those closest to the situation, Alain Locke and Charlotte Osgood Mason sided with Hurston. To date no clear evidence has emerged to settle the dispute. Consequently, we cannot tell how much Hughes adds to the play but even Rampersad acknowledges that* Mule Bone *carries the distinct imprint of Hurston's hand.*

Whatever the circumstances were, years later Hurston seemed sincerely grieved over her break with Hughes. Olivia's situation was not of the scale and drama of Hurston's conflict with Hughes but it would have an impact. Olivia, too, seemed genuinely hurt that the conversation had deteriorated to veiled threats and misunderstandings, rather than elevating to a genuine exchange. Over the years of study, Olivia and I had been drawn into a conversation that was somehow always about the trouble between women and men rather than some more abstract academic ideal. We had been soberly taking risks in order to gain a measure of authority in the conversation only to discover that we must seize the right to narrate one's story. Like power, authority has to be wrested. (That was Hurston's anxiety acted out with Hughes.)

Despite the feeble gestures of support offered by the academic machinery, Olivia managed to grow into a formidable professor and researcher. When Olivia finally speaks up for herself she is a lot like Janie of Their Eyes Were Watching God.

> *Janie took the middle of the floor to talk right into Jody's face, and that was something that hadn't been done before... Ah'm uh woman every inch of me, and Ah know it. Dat's uh whole lot more'n you kin say. You big-bellies round here and put out a lot of brag, but 'tain't nothin' to it but yo' big voice. Humph! Talkin' 'bout me lookin' old! When you pull down yo' britches, you look lak de change uh life. (75)*

By the time Janie turns forty Jody has been insulting her for most of her life. The institution represented in the novel is not the academy; it's marriage but many of the challenges for a woman like Olivia are similar. The aging academic, no longer sure of his academic prowess or of the value those gains have wrought, seeks to silence rather than to engage his unlikely opponent in debate. Finally, Olivia responds like Janie with enough wit (and perhaps enough venom) that she manages to deflate him completely. He'd spent years building himself up at her expense but it only took one tug on a loose thread to unravel his life's work. Bags of skin hung around his frame and Janie exposed him before the eyes of those he thought to deceive. She spoke up for herself and struck back and in one gesture grabbed onto the bone of contention. She claims her "womanhood" and throws Jody off her back, a gesture of liberation as much as it is a changing of the guards. He responds violently. Janie is perplexed: "Why must Joe be so mad with her for making him look small when he did it to her all the time? Had been doing it for years" (77). Janie seems to be unaware of the ramifications of her act.

In fleeting hopeful moments while writing, Olivia had thought he would understand and engage her in a genuine conversation for the first time. I had thought otherwise. He was too invested in seeing himself, if not powerful, more powerful than her to abandon his myths and negotiate with her.

Reading Olivia's critique, I experienced my share of discomfort but I had not anticipated such a personal response from him. He responded with the cold scorn of a jilted lover. I wanted to ask, "When did you step on his winky?" Instead I told her, "Really, Olivia, his response doesn't have much to do with you at all." He was like Jody, confronting the significance of his own mortality: "The more his back ached and his muscle dissolved into fat and the fat melted off his bones, the more fractious he became with Janie" (74). He was hoping to frame his life in terms that would survive him. Then Olivia "took the middle of the floor to talk right into... [his] face." In the novel, "Janie had robbed him of his illusion of irresistible maleness that all men cherish, which was terrible" (75). Had Olivia done any less?

Janie's ability to finally meet him on his own terms marks the beginning of the final leg of Jody's decline. For him, "There was nothing to do in life anymore. Ambition was useless" (76). He had been the big voice of the town and stood on Janie as his pulpit just like he stood on the carcass of Matt Boner's yellow mule.

Throughout the novel the mule has been symbolic for Janie and her plight. Her grandmother had declared, "De nigger woman is de mule uh de world so fur as Ah can see" (14). Her first husband, Logan Killicks tries to make her into a mule to work his land. Naturally, Janie is enamored by Jody's gesture of emancipating the neglected animal. Janie says, "Jody, dat wuz uh mighty fine thing fuh you tuh do.... You have tuh have power tuh free things and dat makes you lak uh king uh something" (55). In buying the yellow mule's freedom, Jody reaches the height of his power. The gesture establishes his power and his benevolence in the town. When the animal finally dies, the town stages a funeral over which Jody presides. He gives the mock eulogy standing atop the body of the mule. While the rest of the town enjoys the display, Janie is forced to remain behind and tend the store. Buzzards circle overhead waiting for their next free meal and are silent witnesses to the mock funeral. After the dragging out, Hurston moves entirely into folklore when the buzzards have their own funeral services for the departed mule that mirrors the one presided over by the townsfolk. In this brief passage, Hurston liberates herself from the constraints of the story as she has told it to this point and allows herself to imagine a place where animals are like us and speak. In this moment the "lie" told as a ritual feast between birds tells an eternal truth that reaches beyond the limitations of fiction.

"Olivia," I asked, "What killed this man?"

Listening in the spaces between the words, Olivia knew how to respond. "Bare, bare fat."

"What killed this man?"

"Bare, bare fat."

"What killed this man?"

In a voice that betrayed neither mercy nor triumph she replied, "Bare, bare fat." *When the buzzards finished picking, nothing was left of the mule except the stuff of legends—no meat, not even baggy sacks, nothing remained besides the unsalvageable bones.*

Works Cited

Boyd, Valerie. *Wrapped in Rainbows: The Life of Zora Neale Hurston.* New York: Scribner, 2003.

Gates, Henry Louis, Jr. *The Signifying Monkey.* New York: Oxford University Press, 1988.

Hemenway, Robert. *Zora Neale Hurston: A Literary Biography.* Chicago: The University of Chicago Press, 1977.

Holloway, Karla. *Moorings and Metaphor: Figures of Culture and Gender in Black Women's Literature.* New Brunswick, NJ: Rutgers University Press, 1992.

Hughes, Langston and Zora Neale Hurston. *Mule Bone: A Comedy of Negro Life.* Edited by George Houston Bass and Henry Louis Gates, Jr. New York: Harper Perennial, 1991.

Hurston, Zora Neale. *Dust Tracks on a Road.* New York: Harper Perennial, 1991. B. Lippincott Inc., 1942.

---. *Their Eyes Were Watching God.* New York: Harper and Row, 1990. 1939.

Kaplan, Carla. *Zora Neale Hurston: A Life in Letters*. New York: Anchor Books, 2002.

Lewis, David Leevering, ed. *The Portable Harlem Renaissance Reader*. New York: Penguin, 1994.

Locke, Alain, Ed. *The New Negro*. New York: Maxwell Macmillan International, 1992. 1925.

Ogunyemi, Chikwenye. *African Wo/man Palava: The Nigerian Novel by Women*. Chicago: The University of Chicago Press, 1996.

Plato. "Theaetetus," *Plato: Complete Works*. Ed. John M. Cooper. Indianapolis: Hackett Publishing Company, 1997. 157-234.

Soyinka, Wole. *Isara: A Voyage Around "Essay."* New York: Random House, 1989.

Stavney, Anne. "'Mothers of Tomorrow': The New Negro Renaissance and the Politics of Maternal Representation," *African American Review*. 32.4 (1998): 533-561.

Thompson, Robert Farris. *Flash of the Spirit: African and Afro-American Art and Philosophy.* New York: Vintage, 1983.

Walker, Alice. "Zora Neale Hurston: A Cautionary Tale and a Partisan View," *In Search of Our Mother's Gardens.* New York: Harcourt, Inc., 1983. 83-92.

CHAPTER 3

HAMBONE

> By faith Joseph, when his end was near, spoke about the exodus of the Israelites from Egypt and gave instructions about his bones.

—Hebrews 11:22

> Do not bury me in Egypt, but when I rest with my fathers, carry me out of Egypt and bury me where they are buried.

—Genesis 47: 29-30

> Hambone, Hambone, Where you been?

> Around the world and back again?
>
> —traditional rhythmic chant

Home is a disruptive place. While we have imagined it to be otherwise, home is perhaps no more of a refuge than the next place. Yet, the idea of being able to return to a place that has witnessed our beginnings is attractive and so the notion of home continues to appeal to us across cultures and over time. Home is a journey characterized by the illusion of repeated encounters in a familiar place. We believe that where we come from says something significant about who we are. But the structure of home rests upon movement away from that very place. Home is a paradox. Its nature is to subsume a body entirely and to expel that same body, while holding out the promise of a return. Like a uterus, its work is total and complete (in the sense of "complement" rather than "finished") when balanced by healthy interactions with an outside world.

For African American women who were uniformly thrust into the role of domestic service, home is distorted past reasonable proportions. The physical presence of the house seemed to balloon well beyond its natural significance. For these women who were often limited to washing, cooking, cleaning, and caring for other people and their children to earn a living, it was difficult to maintain their own homes. Instead, domestic service positioned black women at the intersection where home and the marketplace converge. Historically, the black woman along with the experiences she represented had been viewed as commodities of exchange. Her job was to protect the well being of the vital family inside the home, which according to the logic of the marketplace, was not her own. In a Nigerian context, Chikwenye Ogunyemi writes of the marketplace as a liberatory space for women who command much attention and authority there. While many factors trouble her reading of that space, particularly in light of a twenty-first century global market, her description of the Nigerian market highlights the peculiarities of the African American experience. In the African American context, the black woman's encounters with the marketplace began with the auction block where she was stripped of her clothing, language, liberty, kinsmen, the labor of her hands, and the fruit of her womb. She entered the American marketplace first as the meat that was bought and sold for the pleasure and sustenance of others.

The market put the black vernacular experience on the auction block. Consequently home, for African Americans, was no less troubled than the marketplace. If home is disruptive, constantly working to draw in and to cast out, then consider the impact of the Middle Passage on the African American's relationship to "home." His identity is forged initially by a forced removal from his homeland and shaped by centuries of repeated rejections in this new land of his birth. The African American is a native son who nevertheless, is not offered rights of inheritance. Consequently, the culture conceived in the putrid belly of a ship, which continued to thrive more than a century after standing for the last time upon the block, represents the resilient craftsmen who knew it took more to build a home than a little wood and brick. These practitioners made a home for themselves using whatever was on hand—broken families, scattered beliefs, a few remnants from the drum, painful memories, chance and thrift, snatches of tunes, rice and beans, greens, and just enough Hambone to season the pot.

The Hambone is at once a manifestation of linguistic word play and rhythmic expression that engages the body as instrument, as well as a remembrance of things past articulated alongside the promise of the future. It reinterprets the experience of destitution through the cultural valence of recovery and improvisation. It expresses the paradoxical longings to be both at home and to move outward into the world. The chant is more than child's play. It was created and gained significance during slavery when the resources available to black people were so limited that a single hambone had to be passed from pot to pot. The hambone contained marrow, a rich source of nutrients and flavor that seasoned the food and gave African American Southern cooking its distinct savor. As the bone made its way along its inauspicious journey, some anonymous innovator wondered, "Hambone, Hambone, where you been?" And perhaps another nearby answered the call, "Around the world and back again." Thus the improvisational word play and its accompanying rhythms, created by slapping hands to chest and thighs, signified on the hardships of black domestic conditions.

The Hambone as a cultural innovation prepares the way for what Henry Louis Gates calls the "speakerly text" and so, a character like Zora Neale Hurston's Janie can travel to the horizon and back in *Their Eyes Were Watching God.* Rather than the meat and bones, which were signs of the distress in Hurston's life (discussed at some length in the second chapter), in this novel she cuts to the center of the vernacular tradition. At the heart of *Their Eyes* is a woman whose journey "around the world and back again" reminds her of the bodily experiences of her youth even as she represents the mature knowledge gained by enduring oppressive husbands and ridding herself of the empty pleasures of Tea (and) Cake, which finally threatens to kill her or to drive her mad, in order to find her way home where she can retire and build community through sharing her story. The passage where Janie puts her tongue in her friend's mouth has been much talked about among critics of the text as depicting the value of storytelling and community. But perhaps I might add one point to the volumes already written on the subject by connecting it with the Hambone. Like a hambone, Janie shares and Phoeby promises to continue passing the story from mouth to mouth. And also like a hambone, Janie's story provides nourishment that enriches Phoeby's life and restores health to her body, "Ah done growed ten feet higher jus' listenin'" to Janie's story (Hurston 182). It is in this ability to engage another in a dialogue that the vernacular has the potential to be most transformative. Growing out of the vernacular practices of African America, the Hambone contains the very marrow of tradition.

In this chapter, I consider the ways that African Americans have created for themselves an alternative tradition that resists the tendencies of white, patriarchal society to reduce the black experience to mere privation. In so far as I am able to participate, vernacular practices reinforce my connection to the South. And in drawing the vernacular into the public discourse of the academic marketplace, I am further investing in the lived experiences of my fore parents, exchanging physical labor for the work of the mind. I begin by considering Charles Chesnutt's *The Marrow of Tradition* because this novel, published at the turn of the century by the first major author of African American fiction, demonstrates so many of the tensions that will trouble the work of black authors throughout the twentieth century. Chesnutt's fiction is among the early efforts to translate the rough experience of Southern black life into a more abstract cultural exchange. Chesnutt evokes both the meat and bones of a rich expressive history by merging oral and written practices in *The Marrow of Tradition* and in so doing self-consciously positions his literature at the fulcrum where race and geography are precariously balanced.

  I follow the reading of *The Marrow of Tradition* with a story of my great aunt Clydie. This story is central to my neo-African *oriki orile* —an articulation of a collective history, which is grounded in a particular place, expresses bonds of kinship, and told through multiple voices.

Although the geography has expanded by the time Suzan-Lori Parks sends her characters digging into the Great Hole in History, the African American sense of place as in Chesnutt's formulation is deeply rooted in the antebellum South (even if his novels are set elsewhere). Within the house of the divided South, African Americans imagined bonds of kinship based upon a shared experience of oppression. While African America was never a unified whole, factions within the larger society managed to carve out philosophical communities, which appear in the twenty-first century academy as schools of thought. These schools function like the notion of *ile* in Nigeria. Within the *ile*, women perform *oriki* in the "private" space of the "house"—which functions here as both a family line, as in dynasty (with or without the accompanying exercise of power), and as a material site. This private, public space, then, offers these performers an opportunity to memorialize current experiences even as they "remember" the past within the present moment. In this frame of reference, kinship is based on a line of thinking rather than bloodlines and ties serve to establish a sense of rootedness without subjugating individuals within an overblown patriarchy. Since Chesnutt is a major influence in my intellectual line of descent, my connection to him is as tenable as my connection to my great aunt because we are of the same *ile*.

And here, as in traditional *oriki*, distinct voices speak from different positions. Parts of this story are conveyed in her own words and parts told by other family members in addition to my voice. Clydie represents the will to survive and the significance of giving voice to the vernacular experience. That she is able to speak for herself matters and it matters that I am able to access that story. But how do I tell this story without removing it from its source? I do not mean to suggest that I am looking for a pure line of women—a mythical mother who gives birth to a daughter, who, in turn, gives birth to a daughter. After all, the tale does not come to me directly. It comes to me aslant—Clydie is my mother's father's sister. *Amita* is the Latin root for aunt, which means "father's sister,"[7] so even as it refers to a female relative it also alludes to a father in my maternal line. In this way, Clydie's story is rather like a hambone that signifies the diversity of my cultural inheritance; it comes out of more than one pot. The effort to tell Clydie's story is an attempt for me to find an adequate outlet for my own. In representing her voice I am saying something about the work that I do as an academic that I cannot say otherwise. The attempt is to construct an adequate theoretical framework that can accommodate vernacular experiences that have gone uncodified. By codifying these experiences in these terms I am attempting to bring Clydie's private experiences into the public arena of the marketplace. This marketplace has emerged out of the socio-political factors that gave rise to American colleges and universities. I place Clydie's story in the center of the chapter, between a more traditional literary analysis and my attempt to read her life as text within a broad academic context, because she enables me to articulate the ways that my critical practice is grounded in the vernacular. Like the Hambone, Clydie's story reminds us that we are living in our bodies, suggesting a cultural resiliency that becomes resistant in so far as it continues to nourish subsequent generations of African Americans.

Resistance

> Ef a nigger wants ter git down on his marrow-bones, an' eat dirt, an' call 'em 'marster,' he's a good nigger, dere's room fer *him*. But I ain' no w'ite folks' nigger, I ain'. I don' call no man 'marster.' I don' wan' nothin' but w'at I wo'k fer, but I wants all er dat.
>
> —Charles Chesnutt, *The Marrow of Tradition*

The Marrow of Tradition is, of course, the title of a novel written by Charles Chesnutt, which was published in 1901. The novel is loosely based on the 1898 revolt in Wilmington, North Carolina that resulted in the overthrow of the duly elected government. A caste system developed during the formative years of the nation that denied African Americans the right of citizenship. During Reconstruction, for a brief time following the Civil War, black men were able to exercise their right to vote and some even held political offices. Wilmington was one of the most progressive cities in the South and because they held a majority until the turn of the century, African Americans were able to make tremendous social and political strides. But on November 10, 1898 an insurrection, which had been in the planning for some time by embittered Wilmington residents, violently instituted a series of Jim Crow laws that ruthlessly enforced a code of white supremacy.

Local papers reported the event as a "Race Riot," suggesting that violent behavior and general unruliness on the part of black residents had to be put down by white citizens. While others watching from a clearer vantage in the North reported that whites had seized the city by "revolutionary methods." Only recently has the event been properly identified in official historical records as the nation's only *coup d'etat*. Alfred Moore Waddell, a former U. S. senator, led the carefully planned revolt, which resulted in the ouster of the mayor and city council. An unknown number of African Americans were killed and many of those in leadership fled or were exiled from the city. Waddell was then "elected" to lead the city of Wilmington as he reinstated white supremacist policies that would usher in the era of Jim Crow. In 2000, the General Assembly of North Carolina established a commission that would spend five years studying the social and economic impact of the events of that day. This late development raises questions about Chesnutt's novel. The first, of course, is its connection to the history that has been denied until recently by official channels; which, in turn, raises questions about the role of fiction in preserving records of past events. While the significance of the insurrection as "history" is still being contested more than a hundred years after the insurrection, Charles Chesnutt published a fictional account only three years after the event that offers both truth and insight into the conditions at work in Wilmington, in particular, but more generally at work in the American South at the dawn of the twentieth century.

Chesnutt gathered research for *The Marrow of Tradition* from witnesses, rather than using newspaper accounts or other documented records. His effort to tell an alternative story to that offered by the official history situates his work as an early example of African American literature which would be produced throughout the twentieth century as an effort of recovery. As Gayl Jones would reiterate in *Corregidora*, history could not be trusted to represent the interests of black people: *"They can burn the papers but they can't burn conscious... And that what makes the evidence. And that's what makes the verdict"* (Jones 22). And yet, writing literature seemed to Chesnutt, at least initially, an effective way of exploring his relationship to his contested home grounds. As Chesnutt writes in his journal, May 8, 1880:

> The Negro's part is to prepare himself for recognition and equality, and it is the province of literature to open the way for him to get it—to accustom the public mind to the idea; to lead people on, imperceptibly,

> unconsciously, step by step, to the desired state of feeling. If I can do anything to further this work, and can see any likelihood of obtaining success in it, I would gladly devote my life to it. (quoted in *The Marrow of Tradition* iv)

Even as Chesnutt seeks to align himself with the practices of an elite group of British writers, *The Marrow of Tradition* captures some of the complexities peculiar to the black experience by representing the interconnectedness of the races. Using his epigram as a nod to Charles Lamb, a friend of Samuel Taylor Coleridge, William Wordsworth, Robert Southey, and William Hazlitt, Chesnutt hoped to situate *The Marrow of Tradition* in relationship to the Romantic writers of the early 1800s while simultaneously laying overt claim to his black vernacular heritage. On the one hand, Chesnutt hopes to establish his place within a heretofore European tradition and on the other, he seeks to position himself within the practice of black cultural production. The duplicity of his efforts is troubling but it reflects the conflict inherent in African American identity.

In addition to situating Chesnutt as an ancestor in the African American literary tradition that gives rise to the rich spirit of literary "rememory" of the mid to late twentieth century seen in works like Margaret Walker's *Jubilee*, Toni Morrison's *Beloved*, Shirley Anne William's *Dessa Rose*, Octavia Butler's *Kindred*, and others, Chesnutt enriches his work by drawing on the marrow of the African American literary tradition. Chesnutt's reliance on the accounts of witnesses ties him to the vernacular practices of African storytellers, who passed down the stories that were at the center of their culture. Unlike the history published by white establishments that threaten to starve the black community of resources vital to sustaining a vibrant culture, the oral history that Chesnutt values nourishes the tradition he hopes to preserve in other places as his conjure stories. His conjure stories are written against the back drop of folklorists, the most famous of whom is Joel Chandler Harris and ethnographers like Thomas Nelson Page and clearly demonstrate many of the challenges impacting an African American author of the late nineteenth century. "But his single most important contribution to the unfinished collective project of revision and reconstruction remains *The Marrow of Tradition*." writes Jae Roe. He continues, "Its relevance today comes from the fact that it is, indeed, a 'period piece,' 'a social statement in literature of its time'; the counter-memory recorded on its pages illuminates the historical continuity in our own time of sociopolitical conditions that produced the Wilmington Racial Massacre" (242). Even if it was not popular (and Chesnutt's novels did not sell well) fiction was available to literate African Americans in ways that other social and political avenues were not.

Chesnutt is considered the first major African American novelist. After *The Marrow of Tradition*, however, he would publish only one more novel. Despite his attempt to find himself among the tradition inspired by the great Romantic authors and his desire "to lead people on, imperceptibly," Chesnutt was not so subtle in practice. Chesnutt was so disappointed with his audience's unwillingness to accept the truth of his remembered version that after 1905, he would finally abandon his literary aspirations. To those authors in the late twentieth century who picked up the literary mantle passed down by Chesnutt, fiction held the potential to document experiences that contradicted the cultural myopia that saw blackness only as a void, by adopting and adapting the notion of "blackness"—which is to say a range of distinctly racialized experiences depicting life in America. The work of these latter twentieth-century writers engages an intercourse between fiction and written and oral histories. *The Marrow of Tradition* is really historical recovery, reflecting the tensions of working within and against established traditions. Despite Chesnutt's growing disillusionment he imagines in this novel an African American woman character born of these traditions who will arise with the authority to challenge the existing order by remembering events. Janet Miller prefigures later characters created near the end of the twentieth century like Sethe in *Beloved*, Dana in *Kindred*, Dessa in *Dessa Rose*, and Ursa in *Corregidora* who must grapple with the tensions of the South even if they can find no easy solutions.

Although it may be more clear in nineteenth-century slave narratives, the African American's early foray into fiction does not represent a departure from oral practices as much as it signals an expansion of the vernacular into a broader market. If the vernacular is as much about nativity as it is about the "mother tongue," then the very effort of finding a medium through which a story of being black in America could be told is a manifestation of the vernacular. Consider, for example, the framing of the novel. *The Marrow of Tradition* opens with the risky labor of childbirth and ends with the pain of sudden, premature death. No two human experiences are more sacred or private. In choosing to frame his novel with these two scenes of domesticity, Chesnutt subjugates the public exploits of his main characters, Major Carteret and Dr. Miller, to the private interactions of the home and family. It is in this place, the novel suggests, that we will find the marrow of tradition.

The first chapter titled appropriately enough, "At Break of Day," finds Olivia and her husband, Major Carteret held by the urgent desire that both she and their child should live. It is the same sentiment James Baldwin captures more than half a century later in a play inspired by the murder of Emmitt Till. Baldwin's lead character says after his son Richard has been murdered in *Blues for Mister Charlie* that he didn't know what he wanted his son to do with his life but he wanted him to live. This is, of course, the most basic and most profound wish a parent can have for his son. And the threat confronting black sons in America historically has been far greater than that facing white sons born on these same grounds. Although it is this danger to the wellbeing of African Americans that motivates Chesnutt to write the novel, he chooses to begin with the birth of a white son and to end with the death of a black son.

At the conclusion of the novel a range of black characters including the loyal Mammy Jane and her son, Jerry Letlow, the wrathful Josh Green, and the Miller's young son is dead. The deaths of these black characters reflect Chesnutt's growing disillusionment with the potential for African Americans from any social class to effect genuine social transformation in the new South. But a few white characters die as well, including Mr. Delamere, an old Southern gentleman, Captain McBane, the brute arm of white supremacy, and Mrs. Ochiltree, the domineering, Southern widow. This representation of death alongside the virtual sterility of Dr. Miller, the educated mulatto physician, suggests the uncertainty of the new South and intimates something about the nature of the impediments Chesnutt experienced as an African American author at the dawn of the twentieth century. Although it is less clear in this novel, Chesnutt's fiction depicted the broad spectrum of humanity descended from the South. Eric Sundquist states:

> One could say that his exploration of class and color divisions produced in Chesnutt an uneasy adherence to a 'subculture' that was part of, not separate from, the middle class; the lower class, the 'folk,' and the reminders of slavery itself were

> contained 'somewhere in its consciousness,' just as the folk beliefs of African origin were contained somewhere in Chesnutt's own imaginative reservoir. The tension between the two realms, and the signs of Chesnutt's honest recognition of his moral obligation to keep them united, appear throughout his fiction. (298)

If Du Bois' *Souls of Black Folk* lays the foundation for African American Studies with his proclamation in 1903 that the color line would be the problem of the twentieth century, two years earlier Chesnutt established in *The Marrow of Tradition* many of the terms that would trouble the African American literary tradition over the course of the next century.

By the end of the novel the caricatures of the old South are dead: the mammy, the Uncle Tom, and the brutal white overseer. The black caricatures are killed in the midst of the conflict between the races while trying to return to their white masters. Captain McBane dies at the hands of Josh Green who has waited years to have his revenge for the violence that resulted in his mother's permanent debilitation, even at the cost of his life. Roe challenges other readings of the novel that suggest Dr. Miller is the most noble character in the novel, reading his passivity as impotent in the face of Josh Green's virulent action—reflecting as Roe suggests, "the urgent need—then as now—for collective resistance" (242). From my vantage, that resistance takes shape as a deep and abiding reliance on vernacular practices, which remain at the heart of the African American literary tradition. And for African Americans the vernacular begins in the divided house of the antebellum South.

It is entirely appropriate, then, that we discover the troubled relationship at the heart of the story between the black and white families from Mammy Jane. Mammy Jane is the eternal witness to the Merkell/Carteret family history. Her knowledge is intimate and bodily. Mammy Jane has served the Merkell family for generations and we find her attending the birth of this son just as she served at Olivia's birth. As the family doctor observes, "no one in town had had better opportunities than old Jane for learning the undercurrents in the lives of the old families" (5). Like William Faulkner will later write of Dilsey in *The Sound and the Fury*, Mammy Jane also seems to have "seed de first en de last" (297). Mammy Jane shares the story of the family origins. Olivia is aging and her health as well as that of the baby is uncertain. Initially the hope of a son seems to bring balance and order to a community that is clearly tied together and yet, bears deep psychic scars resulting from years of entrenched racial divisions. His birth, however, is preceded a few years earlier by the birth of another son born to Olivia's half sister Janet. Olivia's agitation over encountering a woman who looks like her dark twin with a son who looks like he could be her son throws her into premature labor, threatening the well being of both Olivia and the unborn son. Repeatedly these sisters are presented as virtual twins—which vexes, Olivia, the white sister and causes Janet, the black sister, to pine for recognition. In the novel, the black woman is figured both as mammy when viewed in relationship to the white child, as is the case with Jane, and Jezebel when viewed in relationship to the white man, which is the case with Janet's mother. Chesnutt redeems the Jezebel character, however, with a marriage license that calls Olivia's righteous indignation (and her claim as sole heir to their father's property) into question.

The novel culminates in an insurrection, loosely based on the episode that occurred November 10, 1898 in Wilmington. But that event is prefigured by a murderous mob, which has gathered for a ritual lynching that is thwarted at the last minute. Nevertheless, the spectacle demonstrates how race works to corrupt even the most honorable of men. The near lynching involves another coupling, which appears in this case as "sons"—would be heirs to the formidable Delamere estate. Early in the novel we get the sense that young Tom Delamere may not be what he seems and as the story progresses we witness Tom's decent as his reputation is undone by his untoward habits of drinking and gambling. In a final attempt to avoid the consequences of his actions, Tom resolves to steal money in order to pay his debts. To defray suspicion, he frames

Sandy, a black man who has worked for the Delamere family for years. Despite the circumstantial evidence, which along with an allegation is enough to rally a mob to the brink of murder, the elder Delamere is insistent that Sandy could no more be guilty of this crime than could his grandson Tom. The irony is quite apparent to the reader and to many of the other characters in the novel. Although his honor compels him to discover the truth, his misjudgment of his grandson's character takes a toll on Mr. Delamere's fragile health. The patriarch lives long enough to see both his honor and his family line unravel. In the end, he attempts to restore his honor by repudiating Tom in his will and installing the faithful manservant Sandy as heir in his place. But the old man is dead, after all, and the South still has no place for noble gestures that might challenge the narrative of a master race. The "blessing" extended to the black "son" challenges the inheritance of not only his white counterpart but the stability of white supremacy of the entire society. In the context of a South, which becomes hysterical when confronted with the realities of miscegenation, the black "son" threatens to usurp the position of the "rightful heir"—who is necessarily white. This pairing of Tom and Sandy along with that of Olivia and Janet depict the complexities of material inheritance that trouble the legacy of slavery.

By supplying evidence that contradicts white supremacist claims throughout the novel, Chesnutt centers the battle over race on material and psychic inheritance. The first crisis averted in the near lynching is paralleled by a monstrous distortion that happens in the form of the insurrection. No one is left unscarred by the uprising. Those who incited the violence thought they could first rouse hatred then direct the fever but it bubbles beyond their control. Language is misunderstood and Major Carteret, like the witches who set in motion a story of death and destruction in the opening of Leslie Marmon Silko's *Ceremony*, is unable to call the words back. The solitary world of the Reconstruction era town is fractured and uncannily splits into the mirrored experiences of Olivia and Janet, (twin) sisters. Throughout, their husbands are counterparts—Miller living in Carteret's erstwhile home, Miller striving to achieve social justice and Carteret struggling to maintain social privilege. The story consists largely of their exploits in and around the marketplace. By the end of the novel, however, the men are clearly doubles. After the upheaval of the riots, they both become like Pontius Pilate, trying to absolve their responsibility for the loss of innocent life by refusing to act when it is within their power to give aid. Major Carteret turns his back on the angry mob he has helped to incite and, as a result, does not see his servant Jerry Letlow who is trying, in vain, to find safety at his side. Dr. Miller's refusal to leave his wife and son's bedside seems more admirable given the circumstances and his personal loss; nevertheless, he too refuses to accept responsibility for Major Carteret's son's wellbeing. Ultimately, their proximity to grief and suffering compels both men to look beyond matters of flesh and bone.

As is the case in the beginning of the novel when we are introduced to Olivia and Janet's story through the third person limited omniscient narrator speaking in conjunction with Mammy Jane's recollections, by the end of the novel, the important work of the marketplace again yields to the attraction of the home and family, and the sphere of the wife and son. When the focus finally shifts from the interior workings of the white home to the inner workings of the black home, Janet becomes like Osun in that she has the potential to heal the rift between rival factions. We enter her home at a critical crossroads, one that intersects life and death, black and white, friend and foe, kinship and alienation. Chesnutt complicates the specter of the mother and her slain son with lingering questions of bloodlines that suggest the cross as well as the crossroads. While Esu is born and given to be the messenger who attends his mother and the other orisha at the crossroads, Janet no longer has a son. He has been killed in the day's uprising. Janet appears with her son in this late scene as a traditional *pieta* read with a black difference. For most of the book Janet is silent but at a crucial moment she appears "like an avenging goddess" and speaks, while her sister "stood in the attitude of trembling suppliant" (211).

Power is inverted and the dark twin speaks with righteous authority, "Will... Go with her!" Will is her husband's name but it reads like the centurion's request of Christ to heal his servant not by his physical presence with him but by asserting His will that he be made well. Jesus's will is sovereign, with the authority to act without the support of even his bodily touch. In this case, Janet's husband is a healer and she has the authority to either send healing or to withhold it, in effect, inflicting further pain. The black mother stands like a "goddess," mediating on her own behalf and by extension in the interests of the larger community. Throughout the novel the narrator and other voices mediate our encounters with Janet. The critical shift to speaking subject occurs for this black female character when the business of men gives way to the immediacy of life and death that naturally accompanies the mundane domestic life. At this moment, her domain is at once common and extraordinarily resistant to external forces that have sought to dictate the conditions under which she might live. Chesnutt concludes *The Marrow of Tradition* with a powerful interplay of social, spiritual, and political potential hinging upon the word of a grieving black mother. These sisters end with hope, hope that they may produce a line that will endure—the one through the hope of another child and the other through the hope of healing for her son. The healing, the novel suggests, is not just physical but also spiritual healing resulting from mending the breech across the racial divide.

Amita

> Dearest Nettie,
>
> The man us knowed as Pa is dead.... Your stepdaddy been dead over a week, she say. When us went to town to hear the will read yesterday, you could have knock me over with a feather. Your real daddy owned the land and the house and the store. He left it to your

> mama. When your mama died, it passed on to you and your sister Nettie.

—Alice Walker, *The Color Purple*

> I've always wondered what happens when you don't got a mother. Without a mother you don't get born. But after birth, what then?

—Suzan-Lori Parks, *Getting Mother's Body*

It was getting late before we arrived at Gail and Deebe's house. The encroaching darkness exhaled cool dew on the back of my neck so my mother and I kept moving. She had not been to Monticello for some time. I had been to Monticello as a young child so I had no real memory of this place. I did not know this lonely Route 11 but I was all but certain that he had sinister motives. He was clearly in league with the darkness, who had marked us as targets. The near-sighted cartographer had not even acknowledged this town on my map. We rode alongside fields, which sometimes were corralled in rough hewn fences or bordered by patches of woods and pecan groves, but they were completely void of signs of the city—lights, street signs, gas stations, fast food stops, 24 hour convenience stores—which would help a modern day traveler orient herself.

Instead, I encountered an anachronism in the landscape, linked to the present by the paved road. In the past that Jasper County, Georgia knew, travelers found their way by looking overhead. On a cloudless night here, the stars chattering in their plenitude would assure you that you were under a different sky than you've ever been before. Both land and sky are ancient here and suggestive of things past. Or perhaps it only appears that way to one who is excavating raw clay and confronting living roots.

Although she grew up in Washington, DC and had not lived in Monticello since she was a young girl, my mother considered this town home. We drove past the one room schoolhouse at Sardis A.M.E., which my mother attended with her two older brothers. The masonry building had worn well. Used by the church for some other purposes now, the building boasted new windows and pvc piping—but more than a trace of the old schoolhouse remained.

We also stopped at the only place I remembered clearly, the graveyard at Prospect Liberty CME. Lilies were in bloom near Hattie (Callie) Goolsby's grave—this is where my great aunt Callie is laid to rest. Callie was the fourth child born to Bell Benton. Willie Gene was the oldest, who was followed by Jesse, next my grandfather, Loyd, and then Callie. Callie was the baby of the family for seven years before her sister, Clydie, was born.

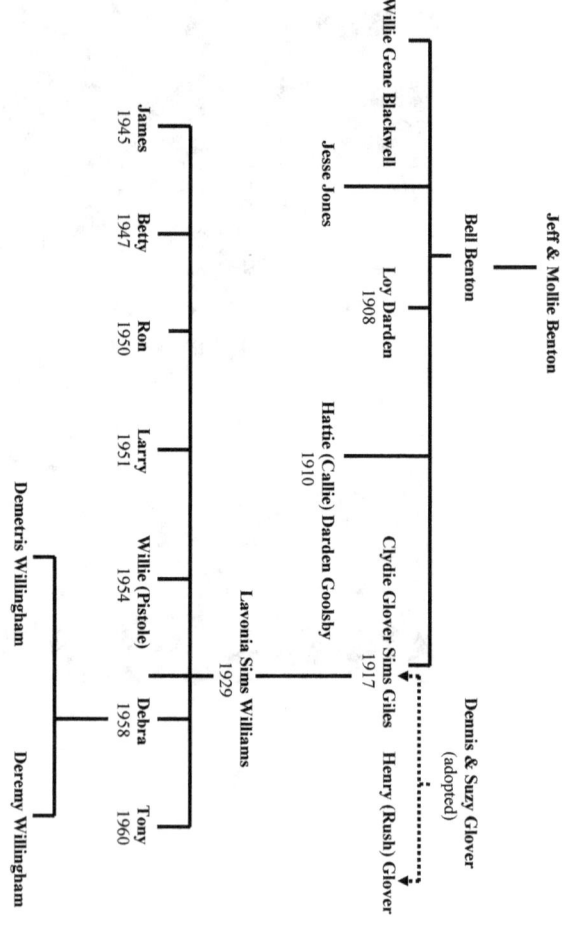

My great aunt Callie loved Callie and took care to pamper herself with pretty things. Drug store perfume introduced her to a room. Callie dolled up pink and purple dresses with dangling plastic jewelry and dazzled me in my girlhood. Before she died she shared a duplex in a government housing complex in Atlanta, with my grandmother's sister, Lizzie, and the two old ladies would sit outside the plain brick building together watching the street activities. Inside, Callie's doorways were obscured by sheets of beads that brought more than a bit of color and rhythm into an otherwise depressing urban design. Crochet dollies adorned the table beneath a glass vase of plastic flowers. As an adult I might have found her taste garish, but Callie's world was magical to a little girl who shared her sense of style.

After Callie died and my aunt Lizzie's health declined, my grandmother had her sister moved to DC where Lizzie lived out the balance of her life. Most of her time in DC was spent sitting in the basement of her niece's Capitol Hill home without a clue where or even who she was. By then Lizzie could lose control of her bowels and still be content enough to greet you with a pleasant smile. If you asked her whether or not she'd had an accident she'd turn the question around, "Is I?"

Nellie Bell Key, Callie Goolsby, and Lizzie Smith around 1981, visiting my childhood home in Maryland.

For some time I was angry about her condition because it seemed so meaningless. After all, my grandmother neglected herself trying to take care of her sister and consequently set into motion a chain of events that would lead to her death within a year of Lizzie's arrival. My great aunt, however, lingered for years in this state of semi-conscious bliss. Having forgotten completely how to care for herself she knew only the most basic rudiments of polite conversation. In time my anger subsided and it was replaced with a kind of admiration for this woman who lived, as my grandmother had wanted her to, despite all of the conditions that suggested she should die. After she finally passed on, we buried Lizzie near my grandmother in Maryland.

The graves in the cosmopolitan setting of Maryland are marked by flat bronze plates that men groom easily with riding lawnmowers. Here reverence for the dead is punctuated by larger than life sized stone renditions of Christ ascending to the Father. People who lived most of their lives practicing rituals that confirmed for themselves their distinctions in terms of class and color even in death segregate comfortably into orders of religion, language and class beneath the seeming permanence of etched words upon stone. The sprawling, manicured acreage of the solemn dead lays in stark contrast to the burial ground at Prospect Liberty CME Church in the Georgian countryside.

Cement poured into crude molds and etched with a stick substitute for marble and bronze tombstones. Wind, rain, summer heat, and winter freezes make quick work of crumbling such stones. Even before the markers erode into faceless debris, green things grow literally out of the shadows with a voracious appetite for space. They care nothing about our rituals and burial practices. Greedily the wild encroaches upon the ripe gravesites, awaiting the carelessness and inattentiveness that generally follow death. No one felt compelled enough to tend after the long dead. Like a tiger, the woods, lurking only a few feet away, wait for memories to fade and the children to move away —people are far less patient than brush.

Cement headstones for Jeff and Mollie Benton at Liberty Prospect A.M.E., Monticello, GA, 2002

The land can be possessive if left untamed and the feeble gestures my relatives made at enshrining the memories of the people who lived and walked the earth were no match for her. She, after all, was living and we were dying. Already, Prospect's older grave sites are guarded by vines. Sticker briers hang from young trees as the earth reclaims her own, preventing those yet living from getting too close to the dead.

My grandmother did not want my mother to bury her in Monticello, which was fine with my mother who didn't believe in carting dead bodies all over the country. Perhaps this is why I was so astonished by Faulkner's Bundren family in As I Lay Dying *who rode Addie's stinking corpse over hills and through high water to bury her in a place some distance from where she lived and died. The gesture seemed so perverse. On the other hand, in the Old Testament Jacob told his son Joseph not to bury him in Egypt and when the children of Israel left their captivity Moses carried Joseph's bones with them. Of course, by the time Joseph buried him next to his wife, Leah, his father, Isaac and grandfather, Abraham, Jacob had been mourned and embalmed—thus sparing all involved the indignity of a parade of buzzards. But the place where they were interred mattered to them and to God.*

The bones of my ancestors, my roots, are buried in Georgia. The realization that the woods are swallowing what suddenly seems so vital is disconcerting. My roots are dying, after all. Those creeping vines and saplings are making roots of me, devouring my life as they climb. I hear an echo of Jean Toomer's Cane *calling with a distinctly southern drawl, "I hold a part of you, you, you...." Toomer's narrator explains:*

> *I felt strange, as I always do in Georgia, particularly at dusk. I felt that things unseen to men were tangibly immediate. It would not have surprised me had I had a vision. People have them in Georgia more often than you would suppose.... When one is on the soil of one's ancestor's, most anything can come to one... (17)*

As I peered through the woods at the headstones, so nearly lost already, I had no visions. But dust and ashes do make fertile ground.

The birth date on Callie's headstone is wrong. The official records at the courthouse and with the Bureau of the Census are not any better. Monticello's birth and death records were kept by careless hands. Perhaps it was merely short sightedness rather than maliciousness on the part of the clerk. Or as my cousin Deebe would suggest, maybe behavior simply had not caught up with the new law requiring states to record births and deaths—black and white.

Deebe: *I figured this out myself when I was tryin' to get a copy of Dad's birth certificate. They got on there that they went around in 1919 on their birth certificate and Dad was eleven years old. I said, "Daddy, when they went around to your grandpa's—he was a Benton—and all ya'll was out there in the yard and them white folks was sayin', 'How old that child so and so? He 'bout 10 ain't he?'" And them folks would answer, "Yessuh." They were so scared to tell 'em, "No," and how old they really was. They put all ya'll down as whatever them white folks said. Just, "Yessuh." They didn't even try to explain it. I believe they just said what them white folks told 'em. 'Cause all of the children was recorded down there 'bout the same age. How can all of 'em be the same age? Someone had to be older than somebody.*

Aunt Clyde down there, too. They got it listed that she older than Daddy. Aunt Clyde says that ain't right 'cause she the baby. They always have said that she was the baby. But Aunt Clyde say they didn't tell it right. I don't believe they told it right. When it come down to it, I don't believe they told it right. They were just afraid to go against their word like we do now. We'll stand up to 'em now. I don't think they did then. Whatever they said, "Yessuh."

Deebe and her granddaughter, Amber in Monticello, Georgia, 2002

The story of unreliable records for African Americans, of course, is old like Thomas Jefferson, dating back to the first time white hand set pen to page on the subject of the African. It has been revised by David Walker who challenged Jefferson to act on his own words and Frederick Douglass in his narrative, Toni Morrison in Beloved, *Sherley Anne Williams in* Dessa Rose, *and Gayl Jones. What shall we do then? Shall we keep our records in a perverse blood-born ledger like that dreamt up by Jones in* Corrigedora—*making generations to bear witness of the past?*

If I believed the headstone, which is no more reliable than those gregarious night-stars, Callie was born in 1912. Actually, she was born in 1910, two years younger than my grandfather and her only full-blood sibling. Looking back, it is difficult to know what occurred to create this family of five children who shared the same mother but only two sharing the same father. Callie's mother, Bell was born in the rural South at the end of the nineteenth century, just one generation removed from slavery. Freedom came slowly to this place. The landscape is still shadowed by the not so distant specter of slavery. People are still living in the quarters that used to shelter slaves, living rent free as long as they work (without pay) for the family who owns the land. Businesses between Monticello and Atlanta still bear the names of large slave owning families and African Americans still occupy the poorest sections of the society. So at the dawn of twentieth century when Bell was scraping out a living from dirt—cleaning it up after some and tilling, sowing, watering, and harvesting for some others—slavery was more real in some ways than freedom.

Bell is probably buried in the same cemetery as her parents, Jeff and Mollie Benton. Unfortunately, the woods swallowed the oldest gravesites long before I began looking for her. Her life is as shrouded as her grave. She married Woodie Darden and in 1910 the couple lived with the four children together on the Price place. Oscar Price was the overseer for one of the more powerful landowners in the Benton family—the white Bentons, not the black. Bell's death severed a vital artery that fed the heart of the family.

Bell caught pneumonia after giving birth to Clydie. In the rural South, poor blacks had little medical care and pneumonia was a very serious condition. In order to survive the fever a person had to fight. Her daughter,

Clydie, was a fighter. Bell was not. By 1917, Bell gave birth to her last child and died. The two oldest boys, Willie Gene and Jesse remained with their grandfather, Jeff Benton. Loy and Callie stayed with their father. Clydie was given to a couple, Danny and Suzie Glover and raised near Mansfield.

Plaque outside the county courthouse in Monticello, Georgia, 2002

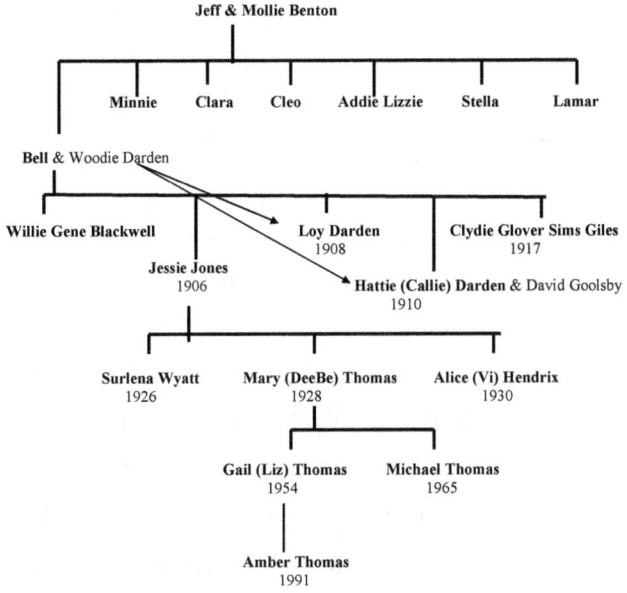

Clydie Giles in Atlanta nursing home after the onset of Alzheimer's disease, 2002

I met my mother's aunt Clydie in Atlanta. Beautiful white hair tucked into pin curls. A pink sponge roller held her bangs. Clydie was eighty-four years old, a slight, pale gold woman. Her sharp features were worn smooth like a rock in a steady cool stream. At that time she lived in an upstairs apartment in her daughter's home along with her great grandson. She leaned a bit on a cane but a lot of the fire that must have characterized her young life was still in her eyes. Clydie announced proudly soon after we arrived that she still drove her car to the grocery store and to church. She told us that she'd drive from Atlanta to Monticello too, some sixty miles, if she didn't think her daughter would kick her ass. Clearly, this woman who had gaping holes in her short-term memory had no business behind the wheel of a car. But I could imagine that she would be difficult to contain. I loved her immediately.

Although she did not know me and could not recall my mother, she brought us into the living room to sit. Aunt Clydie began to entertain us with stories drawn from her childhood painted in vivid detail. All but blind to the events of the past five minutes, her descriptions of events from sixty or seventy years ago sprung up before her eyes like a moving picture. Aunt Clydie's mother died soon after her birth. She was given away by her maternal grandparents because her father was a white man she never knew.

Clydie: When I was brought away from down there with my granddaddy I don't think my mother had been dead but 'bout a week. She died tryin' to birth me, from what this lady told me. I was raised by the people who adopted me.

I didn't go under my daddy's name. My brother Loy was a Darden. Jessie was a Jones; that's my brother. You remember my sister, Callie? She was a Darden. I was a Glover. No, I wasn't no Glover. I don't know what I was. I don't know whether they had me in Darden, Benton, or what. I really don't know.

I was raised by Dennis Glover and his wife, Suzy. They had adopted another little son. My daddy has some other children. Well, he had a daughter—my mother didn't. And he had adopted a son, Rush—which Rush went into Glover, too.

These people that raised me, Dennis Glover and his wife, was good friends with my granddaddy, Jeff Benton. They used to fish and rabbit hunt together. He told me after I grew up, he said, "I went down to your granddaddy's house," See they had been fishing, "and heard a little baby cry."

I said, "yeah."

He asked him whose it was and Jeff Benton told him that I was his daughter's baby and he didn't want me in his house because a white man was my daddy. That was my granddaddy, now. That was my mama's daddy and this man that raised me, Dennis Glover, says to him, "What you gonna do 'bout it? You don't want her in your house?"

"No, I don't." That was my real granddaddy, now, "I don't want her in my house."

So Dennis Glover says, "Well, you want to give her away?"

He said, "Yeah, 'cause I don't want her. Her daddy is white and I don't want no half white chil'ren in my house." You know I hated that old man after that. I never did have no use for him. I didn't 'cause see, I couldn't help it what my mama done.

No, and my daddy told him, "I tell you what, tomorrow me and my wife will be down here to get this baby."

He said he heard this baby back in there crying. My granddaddy told my brother Jesse, "Go on back there and get that hollerin' baby some milk." Jesse brought me outta the room from somewhere and had me a glass of milk and just poured the milk. I'm just hollerin'—choking, strangling, milk just running everywhere.

My daddy said, "Jeff Benton, that ain't right. What's the matter with you?"

"I don't want her in my house."

He said, "Why you don't want her in your house?"

"Her daddy is a white man."

"Who had her? Well, your daughter had the white man, you didn't have him. And she's still your grand!"

"I still don't want her in my house."

Don't you know I didn't have no use for that old man? Noooo, no! You can tell chil'ren things and they don't ever forget it. I never did have no use for him.

My daddy went home and told my foster mother, "I found us a baby."

She said, "What?"

"And we're going to get her tomorrow. She is the prettiest little thing." You see, he knew my grandparents real well.

Mama told him, "Alright," so they went down there and got me.

Clydie is my mother's father's half sister. She was raised only a few miles away so she still had contact with her siblings and on occasion she would spend time with them. Clydie's hatred of Jeff Benton preserved her memory. Since her childhood she knew her grandfather as the man who blamed her for the sins of her biological parents. Rather than care for her, he threw her into the loving arms of her adopted family. Despite the fact that Jeff was responsible for placing her in a caring household, she would never forgive her grandfather.

One explanation for Jeff's strong reaction to the infant Clydie might be that she served as a painful reminder to her grandfather of all that he had lost. Not only had his daughter died following Clydie's birth, the pregnancy itself is of questionable origins. The line separating consensual sex and rape was little more than the difference between a chuckle and a belly-busting laugh among old boys even for white women at that time. For a poor, uneducated black woman there was no difference at all. Certainly women knew through experience what Ella, a character in Toni Morrison's Beloved, *calls "The Lowest Yet"—a white man who satisfied his sexual appetites at the expense of the black woman.*

Ella feels no attachment to the children born of rape and she lets them die. If Ella could find no evil worse than the crimes exacted upon her, perhaps a man like Jeff Benton might have held some disdain for a man like the "The Lowest Yet" too.

Clydie grew up hating Jeff Benton and believing that he had all but thrown her away. Perhaps he had, but he didn't raise his other grandchildren either. He still had his own unmarried children to care for. He kept only the eldest boys, Willie Gene and Jesse, both teenagers who were useful on a farm and sent the others to live with relatives and friends. Loy and Callie lived with their father Woodie. Clydie, the last of his daughter's children, was raised by Dennis and Suzy Glover as their own child.

The only time Clydie expressed a desire to meet her biological father was after she was nearly a teen-ager. Before moving north, he asked her older brother Jesse if he knew how to find his daughter. According to Jesse, he had a sum of money he wanted to leave with her but no one volunteered her whereabouts. "Why didn't you tell that white man where I was if he had some money for me?" She asked indignantly. Then she presented a deep, healthy laugh, seasoned with a slightly ribald wit. Clydie's siblings and even her grandfather refused to help her father make the feeble gesture of fulfilling his parental obligation through a one-time cash payment. She had been disinherited from the time of her birth. Bell's death had left her unmothered and her illegitimacy left her without clear paternity. Consequently, Clydie's very nativity is called into question. Paradoxically, stories such as hers are undeniably born of the American South. While the patriarchal system that has dominated southern society denies any claims Clydie may have to an inheritance as illegitimate, vernacular narrative resists such patriarchal reductions. Despite the fact that she is the quintessential example of "Mama's baby, Papa's maybe," Clydie is far too self-assured to be tragic. It simply never occurs to her that she should not be accepted and she reserved her most volatile contempt for those who seemed to feel otherwise. This aspect of her personality was evident even as a child. Even in the later years of her adulthood, Clydie could play back scenes of her childhood that captured her spirit of resistance.

Clydie: We lived in Monticello, Georgia. I was raised down in there, down below Mansfield. Me and [my brother] Rush went to school. We walked about three miles every morning to school. Rock Springs, I think that was the name of the church where they was havin' the school. And we walked every morning. We had to pass a white school to get to our school. It was down there between Monticello and Mansfield.

You know, I always did hate white folks.

Listen to this. When I was in the first grade, well, me and Rush both were in the first grade. We had to walk pass they school house to get to our school. And in the afternoon when they turned us out, by the time we walked down there they would be coming out. And I would jump on me one of them white folks. I'd whoop me one every evening. Rush would have to hold me. I hated white folks. I hated them.

Whoooweee! Mama whooped my butt. It didn't do no good. I'd go right back the next day.

We had to take our lunch to school in a lard bucket. I tore up all the buckets she had fightin', beatin' them white chil'ren. She started to fixin my lunch in a flour sack! I was a sorry rascal.

I was old enough to go to school now. I was about six or seven years old. I know about all that. I said Jesus Christ! I'd whoop them crackers. I'd grab me one and Rush couldn't get me away from 'em. They changed they hours! Them white folks changed they hours so them crackers could be gone on when we came along.

I'd fight everyday. I'd jump on one every day. I can remember that well.

Barred from attending the same schools as her white counterparts, Clydie displaces her anger onto the children who benefited from the system of injustice. Her daily routs impact more than the children who happen to fall prey to her violence. In response to Clydie's attacks the white school ends its day early enough to avoid these encounters. This picture of my aunt Clydie who was a petite woman and who must have been tiny as a girl bullying enough children to convince school officials to make adjustments rather than to address the actions of an individual child is markedly different than the one we generally imagine in association with the Jim Crow South. It doesn't take a far stretch of the imagination either. In 1915, just two years before Clydie was born, Monticello responded ruthlessly to an alleged assault against the sheriff. After resisting arrest, four members of the Barber family, a father, his son and his two daughters were taken from the local jail and lynched. The newspaper account reads like a comic book sketch (minus the heroism):

THE MONTICELLO NEWS

*"The Monticello News Covers Jasper Like the Sun—
Its Rays Shine Into Every Home"*

ESTABLISHED IN 1881 | MONTICELLO, GEORGIA
FRIDAY, JANUARY 23, 1915 | NUMBER 50

FOUR NEGROES LYNCHED
BY MOB HERE
LAST THURSDAY NIGHT

A terrible sequence to the assault upon Chief of Police, J. P. Williams last Wednesday night, an account of which was carried in these columns last Friday, was the quadruple lynching of members of the Barber family last Thursday night by a mob of unknown parties who overpowered Sheriff James R. Exell in his office and took from that officer the keys to the jail where Dan Barber, his two daughters and one son were incarcerated.

Sheriff Overpowered

Like a clap of thunder from a clear sky a bunch of masked and armed men swooped down upon Sheriff Exell as he sat at work in his office and before that official realized what was happening the keys of the jail were taken from his person and in the twinkling of an eye the mob had swung into a trot to the jail for the prisoners.

A hasty entrance was made at the jail and after taking therefrom Dan Barber and his daughters and son, Ella, Eula and Jesse, the infuriated men hurried the frightened prisoners to a small thicket of pine trees about a half-mile from Monticello on the Hillsboro road where volley after volley of shots informed the citizens of our town that a horrible deed was being committed.

It is needless to say that no one knew from whence the mob came and whither it went after the lynching was over. Men semed [sic.] to have veritably sprung up from the earth and as quickly vanished again.

A Gruesome Sight

The sun rose the next morning upon a hideous scene—the riddled bodies of the participants in the Wednesday night attack upon Chief Williams. The body of Dan Barber, the father, was dangling from a limb, while those of his daughters and son were piled in a heap at the base of the same tree from which swung the ghastly form of the parent.

Operated "Blind Tiger"

For some time Dan Barber and members of his family had been engaged in the illegal sale of whiskey, in addition to operating a disorderly house, and to this place of perpetual crime the city's chief went on the night before to make a search for "blind tiger liquor." His presence precipitated a general melee and the policeman barely escaped with his life. The timely arrival of Sheriff Exell is the reason he is living today. For some minutes Chief Williams fought and plead with the maddened negroes. Disarmed and prostrated upon the floor with Dan Barber upon his body and Barber's daughters peppering him with every available instrument was the plight of Mr. Williams when Sheriff Exell reached the scene.

Citizens Deplore Dead

When it was known that the negroes had been lynched, our citizens were horrified and their denunciation of the crime was prompt and strong.

Mayor Called Mass Meeting

Early Tuesday morning Mayor E. T. Malone issued the following call for a mass meeting in the court house at 2:30 o'clock: "A mass meeting is hereby called to convene at the court house in Monticello, Georgia, on Tuesday, the 19th day of January, 1915, at 2:30 o'clock, p. m., for the purpose of passing appropriate and suitable resolutions concerning the recent lynching in Monticello. All good citizens of the town and county who deplore this occurrence and condemn this lawlessness are requested to be present."

At the hour named above about 206 representative men of Jasper county and Monticello met in the court room and discussed the situation at length.

In the March, 1915 edition of The Crisis, *W. E. B. Du Bois surveys the response to the Barber family lynchings reported in newspapers across the country as part of his ongoing campaign to end such acts. One editorial cites the hypocrisy of a "free" and "just" society that continues to allow such routine outbreaks of mob violence: "Could anything more clearly set forth the inherent right of the white man to govern or the moral superiority of the Caucasian over the African? So long as such shocking evidences of brutal depravity are more or less common in the southern section of this country, the rest of the world may well look upon the United States as a semi-civilized land" ("Lynchings" 225). Under the scrutiny of a national spotlight, the lynchings became the subject of a number of public resolutions after an inquiry by the governor but no arrests were ever made.*

The brutality of the crime as well as the public absolution of the mob demonstrated the prevailing sentiment in Monticello still held to the tenants of white supremacy. Monticello was no Eatonville, made famous by Zora Neale Hurston, where black people could maintain at least the illusion of sovereignty. African Americans were clearly subject to white domination. Nevertheless, as a girl Clydie is a lot like the irascible Zora; she is unwilling to sit on a fence post and watch the world with all its people go by. Undaunted by her slight stature, she was a mess to deal with as a child and no less challenging at the turn of the new millennium. Here sits a fighter—feisty and irrepressible. This character is what I imagined we had that kept African Americans from succumbing to the pressures of the deep South during the height of Jim Crow segregation that would have us hate ourselves so fiercely that we would either be as mindless as sheep or die.

African American writers drew their subjects out of vernacular experiences. More often than not, that experience entailed disenfranchisement, disinheritance, repudiation, and deprivation enforced by white institutions including the judicial system, churches, schools, and families. Even for authors like Ann Petry publishing her work in the 1950s who had no regional ties, the black identity is shaped by the terms established in this harsh southern landscape. Throughout the twentieth century fiction was used to tell the truth of how black people spent their lives. That is why Chesnutt's The Marrow of Tradition, *which shows the picture of a troubling new South, draws upon the same terminology as my great aunt Clydie's story. In both instances, we have the deadly backdrop of mob violence and the government's disinterest in protecting the rights and human dignity of African Americans along with the failure of historical documents to accurately record events. In her story, Clydie resists these factors. But her story might become a mere parody, a cakewalk rendition of the true power violently enacting its will upon the black community, if not for her ability to pass it from her mouth to mine. Clydie's story emerges, then, as more than linguistic wordplay, it becomes like a hambone seasoning and enriching my pot— creating community and reinforcing bonds of kinship. And now that I've gotten a bit of flavor, I intend to pass it on.*

Marketplace

vernacular—*n* 1. The native language of a country or region, esp. as distinct from literary language. 2. The nonstandard or substandard everyday speech of a country or region. 3. The idiom of a particular trade or profession; *in the legal vernacular.* 4. An idiomatic word, phrase, or expression...—*adj* 1. Native to or commonly spoken by the members of a particular country or region. 2. Using the native language of a region, esp. as distinct from the literary language: *a vernacular poet.* 3. Pertaining to, spoken in, or

> written in the native language or dialect. 4. Pertaining to the style of architecture and decoration peculiar to a specific culture. 5. Occurring or existing in a particular locality; endemic: *a vernacular disease.*[8]

Clydie's story resonates with me for reasons I find difficult to explain. But it seemed to me that if I could hear from her some of the details that made up her lived experience then I would have recovered a crucial part of myself, a part I had been missing too long to know even that it was gone. The gaps in her short-term memory were signs of advancing Alzheimer's disease. The plaque that kept her from imprinting my name in her mind was greedily eating away at even these indelible images that have been with her for most of her life. Whatever it was I thought I needed from her lay in the past of her lived experiences even as those same experiences are quickly retreating from view.

That is, of course, the nature of life. It is fleeting. What we capture we hold for an instant and we involve ourselves with it more or less. Life should not be wasted in the moment. It should be spent in such a way that yields a wise return. The challenge comes in investing in those moments that will bring in future interest. These are economic terms drawn from the language of the marketplace. In Ancient Greece, women were not permitted to participate in the public activities of the agora. The marketplace was the province of men. Of course, I am some distance removed in time and space and heritage from the ancient agora, but overt restrictions on black women's participation in the American marketplace were finally lifted in the post-Civil Rights Era—within the short span of my lifetime. Everywhere evidence suggests the lingering effects of those restrictions.

For me, the marketplace is not a place of potentially unlimited gain. Instead it is a place of cultural exchange. It is a place I enter in order to exchange one set of valuables for another. In theory, I bring my intellect, service, and academic skills to the table in exchange for monetary compensation and social and professional standing. In practice, I bring my time and commitment, and I exchange them for a set of academic values that encourages me to adopt the needs of an institution as my own. The market, the place of cultural exchange, is set in opposition to the vernacular experiences of home. But I am hoping that I will be able to transform this place by spending my life differently than African American women have been permitted to in the past. Perhaps I can bring my vernacular experiences into circulation without having to divest my interests. When placed in circulation, life resists the forgetful, disinterested gestures of the marketplace exchange in favor of remembering the people encountered over time. Time passes but the life we shared resounds like a familiar call echoing across a chasm. The echo can linger longer than memory and become caught in a place somewhere between being and knowing. In sharing her story Clydie lends her presence, giving form to the hollow echoes of the past. Her words assign meaning to those distant reverberations still clambering to be heard.

The demands of my own life did not allow me the luxury of a leisurely introduction and prolonged encounters with her. The time we had to sit together was painfully clipped. I had only just met her but she seemed a vital link to my past. And I felt that without knowledge of her I was denied access to part of my future. Like a sankofa, I thought I might move forward by looking back. That bird flying between my past and future is fed, in part, by Clydie's vernacular story. I listened with delight to her tale of attacking random children who were leaving the segregated white school. She had been forced to walk past their school in order to reach the one designated for black children. She chose to hate them rather than to envy them and hate herself. Clydie used what she had in her hands as a weapon—which happened to be a makeshift lunch pail. Every day she would target a child upon whom she pounded out her frustrations. Then she would go home to receive her punishment. Punishment is no deterrent for one determined to resist.

Clydie rejected the false benevolence of an institution that limited her education and assigned her to a lower social station. She would go to school and learn but she would also register her complaint through daily attacks upon the first white child she could grab. By what right had these children been privileged over her? Their lives, she was told through any number of ways, were more meaningful—a message reinforced by these separate and unequal institutions. Clydie challenged the notion that held her to be any less than anyone else through routine physical altercations. Then she goes even further by defining the encounters and its impact on her own terms. Her delight is apparent as she exclaims, "They changed they hours!" She had forced change within an institution that had ostensibly denied her significance. By first fighting back and then by telling the story as an alternative to the dominant narrative of white supremacy Clydie lays claim to the vernacular tradition of storytelling as a tool of social resistance. Her story of self-worth gains value within a society built upon her degradation even as similar stories have been repeated throughout the South in various manifestations over the years. Perhaps that is the power of the vernacular, an ability to resist passing away so long as it is spoken, repeated, revised.

In a Nigerian context, the vernacular derives from a dynamic history of oral practices described by Chikwenye Ogunyemi as originating around the mother's cooking flame in a moonlit compound. In the European tradition, the vernacular became known as the "mother tongue" because it was the language spoken within the home. It is opposed with Latin the literary language, the "father tongue," that is the language of the marketplace. In both traditions, then, the vernacular is bound up with notions of motherhood and nativity. Without the luxury of a stable hearth, the African American vernacular has a peculiar pedigree having been conceived within a set of circumstances that tends to un-mother even as it works to disinherit. In this context, the vernacular is that language common among Southerners that is able to speak the lived experiences of their private selves.

That is why Clydie's narrative is vernacular despite her estrangement from her mother and her maternal family at the time of her mother's death. The absence of her biological mother disrupts the natural opposition of the interior, private world of the home, with the exterior, public arena of the father. Race enters to complicate the simple dichotomy of inside and outside, mother and father, female and male, by introducing black and white as terms with cultural currency. Unfortunately, the oppositional relationship between black and white, female and male, mother and father, suggests their codependence without an accompanying reconciliation. The black mother dies and the white father disappears into the anonymity afforded by his social privilege. While the mother becomes the prototypical captive —"captive" in the sense used by Hortense Spillers —demonstrating through death the black body's failure to nourish and sustain life, the white father is allowed to transcend the limitations of his body and enter as a full participant into the public place of the market. The absence of a clear bodily presence of either (black) mother or (white) father leaves their racial designations free to issue symbolic directives. Clydie's blackness becomes, in effect, a sign of the mother; conversely, her whiteness is read as a sign of the father. By extension, the social practices that mark an individual as black are feminized in the context of a white masculine dominated world. As a sign of failure, blackness then becomes ironically dependent upon whiteness for restoration within the public arena.

Conversely, the white male dominated marketplace is deeply invested in seeing itself as powerful and so relies heavily upon the notion of blackness as a sign of degradation and primitiveness, if not feminization. Despite the fact that claims of white superiority were reiterated throughout nearly all areas of society, many like Charles Chesnutt saw the fraudulence of such claims. Eric Sundquist writes, "Chesnutt understood from intimate personal experience... that theories of segregation amounted to no more than a kind of superstition.... the philosophy of race purity and the laws of segregation were part of the white world's conjure..." (393). White society, Sundquist suggests, dedicates a considerable amount of resources to constructing and maintaining an elaborate mythology based on race. And these beliefs, like the African American practice of conjure or the African notion of *ashé*, had the power to make things happen. White society erected laws denying black access to social liberties based on their beliefs and as a result African Americans lived in an apparently "separate society" for centuries.

In his critique of the society of which Chesnutt wrote Sundquist continues, "Given the irrationality of segregation and the widespread hysteria about miscegenation, both of which long outlived Chesnutt, the more important question... ironically proved [by *Plessy v Ferguson*, the Supreme Court ruling legalizing the policy of "separate but equal"] was: Who can *appear* to be a white man?" (393). In the logic of the Jim Crow South people can tell just by looking the kind of work for which one is suited. Black people were assigned menial tasks that did not disrupt the illusion of white supremacy. They were taught to work with their hands, feet, legs, and backs to earn a living through serving the white community. As a result, segregation and other factors discouraged black people in general, but especially girls like Clydie, from venturing too far into the marketplace, pushing them, instead, toward the field, the Northern factory, or the home. Even as participants in the marketplace, for much of the twentieth century black women tended to be restricted to the kind of domestic work at which Clydie labored for most of her life. She worked on her hands and knees scrubbing floors, standing on her feet before a stove, keeping house for white families in and around Atlanta. This kind of work that involves the body is the impetus for African American vernacular. Spirituals began as sorrowful moaning that masked the defiant will to escape the toils of slavery. "The blues," Ralph Ellison explains, "is an impulse to keep the painful details and episodes of a brutal experience alive in one's aching consciousness, to finger its jagged grain, and to transcend it, not by the consolation of philosophy but by squeezing from it a near-tragic, near-comic lyricism" (129). Likewise, Clydie's narrative develops from the bodily experience of growing up black in rural Georgia during the early twentieth century.

The mere fact that Clydie must walk past the school where white children are taught to get to the black school emphasizes the physical realities of segregation. If segregated schools were designed, at least in part, to persuade us that black bodies could be put to better use than pursuing more academic endeavors, then Clydie subverts that notion by attacking white children. Physical violence reminds white people (and perhaps even reassures Clydie) that they have bodies too. In this story, the body becomes a site of resistance as Clydie strikes out against the terms of her oppression. Before she is able to tell her story, Clydie has her body. Her connection to her body is primal and she uses it at a young age to express her resistance to an unjust system. On the other hand, her narrative is a mature articulation, a recasting of formative moments in her life. Although the vernacular expression grows out of Clydie's bodily experience of her childhood in rural Georgia it is a considered reflection that helps explain how she makes herself at home within the context of a hostile environment.

In this case, as with the Nigerian and European examples, the vernacular has a lot to do with home. Initially, I was drawn to the vernacular story in my academic pursuit of "home." In 2000, my single-minded quest for home took me to Atlanta where I was doing research. That's when I met my great aunt

Clydie. I went to document her oral narrative. My intent was to bring Clydie's narrative into the academic marketplace. I wanted to link my research with a pedagogical practice drawn from a specific cultural context. Clydie's narrative seemed to offer me a way of acknowledging the roots of my praxis, which is grounded in an experience outside the authority of traditional academic practice. By choosing to cultivate this link rather than to graft myself to a prescribed academic station I was actively resisting conventions for teaching and research already set in place. Really, it wasn't much of a choice. Those conventions were so rigid as to feel painfully constricting to me at the time. I was not invited into the culture of exchange with shares equal to my counterparts entering the market at the same time. It seemed imperative that I mine my experience for its rich cultural heritage if I was to participate in the exchange on more equal footing. My heritage could offer me the intellectual capital academic training had not. So I looked to my mother's aunt Clydie, one of my oldest living relatives, as a means of determining the academic value of how African American women spent their lives.

Clydie spent her life as a domestic worker. She represents the vast majority of black women of her generation who were discouraged from venturing beyond her prescribed position in the marketplace. In effect, they were encouraged "to stay home." This message was perpetuated by limited employment options and reinforced by the paternalism inherent in the system of segregated education. White philanthropic support following the Civil War led to the establishment of segregated schools including institutions of higher learning to train a newly emancipated people to be a productive workforce. Even so, most black girls like Clydie never graduated from high school and those privileged few who went on to the industrial and normal schools established throughout the South were usually channeled into nursing or teaching. Although the 1954 case *Brown v the Board of Education* in Little Rock Arkansas effectively sounded the death toll for segregation in America, in 1955 public school teachers in Georgia began signing agreements not to teach in an integrated class. Of course, all of this occurred well after Clydie had stopped her formal education. Jasper county schools would not yield to desegregation until 1970, following a court order threatening to suspend federal funding if the state's public schools did not comply with the 1954 ruling[9].

The latter half of the twentieth century witnessed the dismantling of segregation in nearly every segment of the public arena and once the old order finally began to topple, one-room schools like the one Clydie attended at Rock Springs were among the first to fall. Integration made the under-funded black schools nearly obsolete. Nevertheless, Historically Black Colleges and Universities (HBCUs) remained as vestiges of Reconstruction Era academic practices. Such institutions might be considered relics if not for the fact that even in the twenty first century, these schools continue to produce a significant portion of the nation's black college graduates. When I returned to my alma mater to teach, the department of English produced more African American graduates in English than any other school in the country. And HBCUs remain the source of the vast majority of African

American undergraduates who go on to complete PhDs.[10] In the post-segregation nation, black schools are manifestations of those aspects within our society that resist integration. These aspects are represented by that spirit that survives in Clydie's tale of her childhood rebelliousness, which complies with the fundamental demands of segregation even as she violently resists. Segregation was implemented in an effort to reinforce the illusion of white supremacy but it continues to be maintained through these schools, in some measure, as an act of defiance. This is why I chose the HBCU twice: first as a student seeking asylum from the racism that plagued my childhood and again as the place I would begin my career. Such gestures have been tolerated because, like a six-year-old girl acting out her frustrations, the larger system of power is not in any real jeopardy. With a few minor alterations, the white supremacist machinery adapts to these modest acts of rebellion and maintains itself largely unaffected.

The university is at its base a patriarchal institution developed and supported as a means of preparing sons to lead in all areas of the market. Women, African Americans, Latinos, Indigenous peoples, and Asian Americans have made a place for themselves within the university system in opposition to this fundamental framework. When Frederick Rudolph published his authoritative study *American College and University: A History* in 1962 he was able to do so with obvious misogyny and a blatant refusal to consider African Americans (or any other non-white population) at all. His thorough investigation of the history of higher education in America reflects the institutional bias to white men more generally.

Of course, as the university developed in America it never embodied its ideals. The four-year institution was founded on the principle of offering students a common experience. Life in the dormitories, classrooms, and sanctuaries were to be held in common so that a father would know the kind of education his son was receiving. Collegiate preparation was about the transition from boyhood to manhood. Initially, Latin and Greek were the language of the erudite in America, demonstrating the clear paternalism between Europe and the young nation. As the university community diversified (broadened to include white men of a range of class and social backgrounds) during the nineteenth century, Greek-letter fraternities began to emerge on campuses in an effort to delineate in a more complex social landscape the "Greeks" from the "barbarians." From the outset the university was exclusionary and as such anti-democratic. As commerce began to displace morality as the most significant national industry, the university adapted to the changing norms. The influence of the Great Awakening, that gave rise to many of the colonial institutions through fierce denominational rivalries, would fade as institutions of higher learning became the proving grounds of the Enlightenment. For the university to remain relevant it had to adapt its elitist practices to match the culture of exploration, particularly within a country founded on principles of religious tolerance and diversity.

The post Civil War era was a time of rapid cultural change across the academic spectrum. Without an entrenched class structure the academy flourished within an industrialized nation. Gerald Graff suggests that by the 1870s the university in America was moving away from the hierarchical European model to a more democratic commerce driven institution. Most educators recognized that the university's survival depended upon their ability to compromise with the "'vulgarity' and 'conceit' of the new business classes" (Graff 22). This compromise appeared as the "coverage model" of education that managed conflict over what and how something should be taught by "*adding* another unit to the aggregate of fields" (Graff 7). Nearly any course of study could be adopted into this model without fundamentally altering the core values of the institution. Primary emphasis remained on educating white men until the people acting within the Civil Rights Era forced the University to justify its practices within the context of a free market. In its ruling on *Plessy v Ferguson* the Supreme Court proved to be wrong. Separate was not equal for women or African Americans.

Even after the bloody fraternal battles of the mid-nineteenth century, race remained a non-issue on the majority of American college campuses for the next hundred years. According to Rudolph, the Civil War was an incontestable demonstration of the resilience of the young nation. Rather than balkanize into a set of smaller states, America continued to expand. That the Civil War happened to "settle the slavery question" warrants but passing mention. The fact that he is writing his history of the American university amid the lingering conflicts of the unresolved consequences of the nation's "slavery question" seems to escape his notice. This study is published just one year before Martin Luther King, Jr. leads the March on Washington and John F. Kennedy is assassinated and four little girls are killed in the bombing of the Sixteenth Street Baptist Church in Birmingham, Alabama—and less than a decade since Emmitt Till's life proves to be worth less than a whistle; Medgar Evers is murdered in his driveway; Rosa Parks refuses to stand and sparks the Montgomery bus boycott; and the Supreme Court orders the integration of schools. Racial strife concerning social inequities is at the forefront of national consciousness yet African Americans are absent from Rudolph's academic landscape. When African Americans began integrating Rudolph's university, black studies departments were developed to accommodate their interests (as were women's studies, Chicano studies, queer studies and any number of other departments to appease the demands of an increasingly diverse academic community). Mirroring the concerns of the larger society, race, rather than class, became one of the flashpoints for the twentieth century campus in America. The academic landscape changed dramatically during the middle years of the twentieth-century, reflecting changes within the larger socio-political arena.

    Blackness had been conceived within a historical frame of reference wherein outcasts had to cross a span as wide as an ocean in order to re-establish themselves in a *new* world. Descendants of Europeans seeking an escape from religious and social persecution like the Pilgrims and the Puritans and the debtors expelled from England who established the colony of Georgia came to believe their whiteness was a sign of inherent superiority. Immigrants to this New World used black people as scapegoats to rid themselves of guilt and sin. In England they might have been convicts, but in America they were white. Whiteness became a sign of all things good and wholesome while blackness was seen as a sign of degradation and evil. It took nearly 250 years after debtors from England established Georgia, the colony that would become the state of my mother's birth, for black to become beautiful. In the 1960s blackness was reborn as black power after centuries of struggle. Afros and raised fists were signs of the difference of a new generation of social activists who rejected white ideals in favor of Black Nationalism. In this way, African Americans sought to re-envision their sense of place and home by acting in the more expansive terms of nationhood. They embraced Africa as mother and the distinct style of the black vernacular marked the new terrain. Academic centers devoted to the study of African and African American culture were monuments to the success of civil rights activists battling for black pride during the mid-twentieth century. Nevertheless, adopting and adapting blackness as a sign of identity is paradoxical. The gesture is simultaneously extremely resistant and intensely compliant.

Arguably, the changes historically white institutions made in response to the social activism of the twentieth century did not encourage innovation in the traditional curricula as much as it worked to co-opt oppositional factions. Just as nineteenth century educators discovered, the modern university had to adapt to a changing marketplace. Adaptation, however, did not necessarily bring about a substantial change in values. The institution generally assigns discourses like those centered on race or gender a caveat within the university system that is arguably more efficacious at pacifying and containing dissent than at opening up a forum for meaningful exchanges. The coverage model utilized by American universities continues to promote the kind of solipsism found in academic practices that reinforces claims of white, male supremacy by compartmentalizing opposition into increasingly fractured cells. These cells do not readily encourage growth and change within dominant culture. Rather, they enable the institutions to continue without significant alterations to the value system by giving African Americans and women, in addition to other disenfranchised populations, room to work within a set of prescribed limitations. Schools peddle prestige won through the extended practice of exclusion and appease the strongest voices of dissatisfaction with tenure and promotion. Despite their apparent productivity, by ghettoizing the academic work of those focused on African American culture into generic black studies programs, these schools may be even less effective at transforming discontent into active resistance than the HBCUs.

From its inception, the HBCU has been emblematic of America's response to diversity in education, demonstrating the way the institution has ensured that academic diversity remain subjugated to white paternal authority. The HBCU was conceived during a time when separate, unequal institutions were created as a means of containing and controlling a black populace while fostering the illusion of white authority. HBCUs have been part of the academic terrain since they first appeared in the aftermath of the Civil War when hundreds of thousands of African descendants were freed from the drudgery of mindless toil. At the center of the national effort to rebuild the union stood the need to define the nation's racial identity and a crucial part of that process was shaped around Negro education. For more than a century the HBCU offered the only opportunity many African Americans had to earn a college degree. In recent years the HBCU has been dealt significant blows as educators, politicians, and citizens debate the relevance (and legality) of such institutions post segregation. Although many HBCUs have not weathered the changing climate, others have maintained their commitment to meeting the academic needs of black people.

The HBCU struggles to break away from its provincial past and its designation as a trade school with little intellectual rigor. In *A History of American Higher Education* John Thelin offers a typical contemporary critique of HBCUs:

> for most of the 110 black colleges, whether public or private, endowments were low, faculty workloads heavy, laboratories antiquated, libraries understocked, and the future uncertain. Perhaps these

> institutions did educate a cohort of young adults and socialize them into the middle class, including professional ranks. But they did so in a largely undistinguished fashion.... And when the most prestigious and affluent white colleges, such as the Ivy League, started to make a concerted effort to recruit and provide financial aid for academically strong black high school seniors, the traditionally black institutions were placed at an additional disadvantage in the competition for talent. (306)

However unmerited, HBCUs still have a reputation, in some circles, as schools for (black) people who are unable to compete within a broader pool of (white) applicants. Perhaps this explains why even today the same government administrations that attack the policies in place to assure racial diversity among the student body of major research institutions is willing to set aside specific funding for HBCUs[11]. Of course such critiques are dismissive of the tremendous social benefits offered by the experience of matriculating at an HBCU that are difficult to measure.

The HBCU has been claimed by today's students and faculty as a retreat from many of the overt and implicit demands of mainstream institutions. Schools that are populated by a majority of whites are often experienced by African Americans as hostile environments that seem to alienate rather than nurture the black identity. On the other hand, the HBCU presents itself more or less explicitly as a home of sorts. It has a rich tradition of homecomings, inflected with particular significance especially when considered in relationship to the larger social context. As a black home place, the HBCU becomes a familiar, insular community within an expansive academic market. By making blackness endemic to the academic experience the HBCU can be read as an extension of the vernacular, validating and containing a private black experience even as it promises entrée to the broader marketplace. The opposition between the HBCU and other schools when imagined in terms of interior versus exterior spaces and private versus public experiences mirrors the dichotomy of the mother language of the home and public literary language of the father discussed previously. In this schema, the outside world can be hostile and painfully disinterested; but the HBCU becomes a "safe place," like those suggested by Patricia Hill Collins in *Black Feminist Thought*, wherein students (and faculty) are allowed to be "black."

The vernacular, then, is reinforced on a number of levels. On one level it appears as the private language of the black mother spoken within the home community. It reappears through the politicized embracing of Mother Africa and again once blackness is adopted by African Americans as a sign of identity. Finally, the HBCU as it has been established and sanctioned as a "black place" is yet another manifestation of the vernacular. Moreover, the HBCU reads as a "home" when viewed in opposition to the broader academic marketplace and, of course, the vernacular is intrinsically tied to the home. When I consider the vernacular in relationship to my decision to do my undergraduate work at an HBCU and then to return as a member of the faculty (of my alma mater) the amount of redundancy occurring in my life amplifies my academic concern with "home" to nearly social dysfunction.

For me, home is not a disinterested metaphor. It is the term that has guided all of my early research. I studied the representation of home in African American literature with the fury of a scorned woman. I was driven to study home, as if understanding the intimate workings of home could unlock the terms of my oppression. Home is the place given to women to tend to the affairs of the family. Home keeps women away from the business of men. Home is woman's work.

I have often said that I chose the subject of my research in order to merge two disparate worlds: my personal life and my professional life. If I had not found a way to do so, I am certain that the former would have completely swallowed the latter. How does one do all of the tasks assigned to a wife and mother associated with homemaking and pursue an academic degree? The cooking, cleaning, mopping, washing of dishes, washing of clothes, folding, ironing, and grocery shopping. Not to mention the story times, bath times, bed times, play times, time outs, potty times, homework times, and quality times. If I had a room of my own, it would simply be another thing to clean.

I imagine myself as an embittered, old woman taking out her frustrations on her husband and her children, lamenting indefinitely deferred dreams. I can see the emaciated legs drawn too long for the bloated frame of her body. Like some cousin once removed from Paul Laurance Dunbar's caged songbird, she'd squawk out epithets through her beaked nose at those passing near her windows. Whistles pressed through her snarled lips turned into curses. Without a suitable outlet for my academic ambitions, I would slowly shrink into that woman. My home was bullying me into feeding all of my desires to it.

In turning my attention toward unpacking the spatial politics at work in the place of home, I hoped to overthrow the tyranny it held over me. Even while my home fed and sheltered, it withheld and constrained. Yet, I could not succumb to the romance of leaving home because home is as much a product of our imagination as it is a physical site. We bear our homes in mind no matter where we go. If I was bound to this place, then I decided to commit myself to the task of finding out how and why.

Like a termite, I worked from the inside, eating away at the structure of home and hoping that I might be able to shift the foundation. And if not, that I might be able to reposition myself in relationship to the dynamics that work to control my life. I imagine the fact of having obtained a degree and an academic appointment signifies that my insurgence achieved some measure of success. Home is the one place that has been able to accommodate my scholarship, my teaching, and my family life.

Toni Morrison may well be right in her 1997 keynote address to a conference on race in America in naming home as a site where the despotism of race can be overthrown. While the tendency of race is to attach conditions to the terms of human interactions, home tends to receive its own unconditionally. Home is familiar and fosters a sense of belonging. This is not to suggest that home is untroubled. Home is besieged with contradictions that make it as fanciful, mythical, or distant in some ways as an amusement park, utopia, or heaven. However, unlike these other places, home grows out of personal experiences and even if we do not believe we have ever been there, "home" appears to be within reach.

Morrison ends her address optimistically, focusing specifically on the issue of race studies in the academy. We gather from her words that such work, when done introspectively, can produce great benefits. "Our campuses," she maintains, "will not retain their fixed borders while tolerating travel from one kind of race-inflected community to another as interpreters, native guides. They will not remain a collection of segregated castles from whose balustrades we view—even invite—the homeless. They will not remain markets where we permit ourselves to be auctioned, bought, silenced, downsized, and vastly compromised depending on the whim of the master and the going rate" (Morrison 11). To invest too heavily in securing the border that separates the campus from its surroundings jeopardizes the integrity of individual academics and calls the viability of our institutions into question.

In fact, as Morrison suggests, we have already begun dismantling many exclusionary practices. The borders of our campuses are kept open under the banner of community outreach, service learning, business partnerships, upward bound, and innumerable other such programs. We pride ourselves on our ability to become a part of the neighborhoods in which we reside. Yet, the authority of race studies is necessarily challenged by the communities "outside" our campuses whose interests it purports to represent. Morrison suggests that unless we envision ourselves as "straddling opposing worlds" or as participants in "escapist flight," academics risk losing credibility within the larger community (Morrison 12).

The metaphor of "home" is not arbitrary in my work. Instead, I came to study representations of home in African American literature as a very deliberate act of resistance. I was consciously seeking to understand the terms of my oppression. In a very real way, I knew that the oppression I was experiencing had a lot to do with "home." It's only now, after I have come to an academic knowledge of the place of "home" that I can read it in a larger context. Home is a place African American authors long for in literature but it is also a place within the academy. After all, my academic inquiry began at an HBCU. I chose to attend a black college in an effort to escape the racism that plagued my experiences with formal education through high school. I rejected the designation as "different"—which I heard nearly every time I shattered a stereotype held by some white kid I went to school with— seeking instead to be immersed in a community that shared a common black experience. But maybe my gesture had not been one of defiance. In choosing to attend an HBCU, had I become another black girl following the demand not to venture too far from home? And in returning as a member of the faculty mildly obsessed with the study of home, perhaps I had become an agoraphobic, altogether afraid to leave the house. Susan Bordo writes, "The pathologies of female protest function, paradoxically, as if in collusion with the cultural conditions that produce them, reproducing rather than transforming precisely that which is being protested" (99). In this work, I see myself rattling the bars that cover my windows. They were put there to keep out the dangers lurking outside but at sunrise when I see the shadows they cast upon my walls I am not sure that they protect me at all. Home can be a prison house. Perhaps I am an agoraphobic, so afraid of the meat market that I am struggling now just to leave home.

My pursuit of home has always been a response. Not so much a passion emerging from within as much as a reaction to pressure from without. I have repeatedly characterized this theme that runs through my scholarly endeavors as initiated in my desire to study the object of my contempt. It has been liberating to understand the object of my contempt—the dynamics set in place to keep me bound. But perhaps I have bought into an illusion of liberty—the illusion that thoughtful, innovative research about a particular subject that adds to our body of knowledge is enough to actually liberate me. I have learned the science at work in the place of home that imprisons. I know now the physics, the spatial politics, the architecture, the dynamics that keep an African American woman like me in her place. I have done good research that forwards understanding generally and personally about why the bars that hold me hold me. But that knowledge does nothing in and of itself to remove the bars.

The last time I visited my aunt Clydie she was in a nursing home located near the campus of Emory University, in the neighborhood where she had preferred as a younger woman to find employment as a housekeeper. After going inside, my mother and I had to wait for a nurse to let us through a large door. Clydie lived in the portion of the home designed for those who needed extra safeguards to keep them from wandering off. I didn't expect her to remember us now that the Alzheimer's had progressed to the point that her family found it necessary to move her to this facility, but it was upsetting to see her level of dementia. For most of the conversation she was fairly engaged, still willing to reminisce about her childhood. She allowed me to take a few photographs before informing me that I had taken enough.

Her eyes had grown a little more distant and she wasn't quite as ready with her laugh. Someone had cut her hair too short to have to worry about rollers. And rather than the feisty old woman I remembered who laughed at her uneven balance while still refusing to use her cane, the beads she wore around her neck made her seem more like a child. The whole time we spoke Clydie was running a set of keys through the fingers of her left hand. My mother asked, "What do those keys belong to?"

"To my car," Clydie responded. "You know about a week ago someone stole my car. Just took it right out Toots' driveway." Toots is the name she calls her daughter, whom she lived with before moving here.

"Are you planning on going somewhere?" I inquired.

"Soon as they bring me my car. My grandson told me they found it. They got it at the house and they gone bring it over when Toots come. Then I can go where I want." The keys moving furiously around her fingers. We *sat for a while and I asked her if I could take another photograph. Clydie refused. We sat. "You talked to Toots?"*

"Yes. That's how we found you. She told us how to get here," my mother responded.

"Toots is coming to take me home today. They gone bring me my car and pack me up and take me home," the keys moving in her hand. Another resident, an elderly man, walked over and mumbled something unintelligible and I didn't know how to respond. Clydie rocked a bit on the love seat and pushed herself up with her still able knees. She walked closer to him, "What's that?"

He mumbled incoherently. "Look can't nobody understand you when you talk like that." She turned away with obvious frustration. She gestured toward him, "That's Toots' husband."

"That's not Toots' husband, Aunt Clydie," my mother informed her.

"Yes it is. You don't remember him?"

"Yes I remember Toots' husband but that's not him."

"Who is it then?" *Keys working furiously through her fingers.* *"They coming today to take me home."*

Soon after, we said our goodbyes. We walked to the door and waited for a nurse to let us out. The large door opened, we passed through, then it shut with the sound of electronic switches and locks. While I could no longer see them, I knew the car keys were still moving furiously through Clydie's fingers. They belong to her in a way that this place and everything else in it never would—a sign of yesterday's promises. Through the fearsome fog of Alzheimer's Clydie still remembers to hold on to her keys. They have not been stolen and they remain her best hope of finding her way home. I left her there waiting for her daughter to come and rescue her. Her fingers fighting to keep it all in perspective.

in loving memory
Clydie Glover Sims Giles
1917-2007

Works Cited

Bordo, Susan. "The Body and the Representation of Femininity," *Writing on the Body: Female Embodiment and Feminist Theory*. Ed. Katie Conboy, Nadia Medina, and Sarah Stanbury. New York: Columbia University Press, 1997. 90-110.

Chesnutt, Charles W. *The Marrow of Tradition*. 1901. Mineola, NY: Dover Publications, Inc., 1998.

Ellison, Ralph. "Richard Wright's Blues," *The Collected Essays of Ralph Ellison*. New York: The Modern Library, 2003. 128-144.

Faulkner, William. *The Sound and the Fury*. 1929. NY: Vintage International, 1990.

Graff, Gerald. *Professing Literature: An Institutional History*. Chicago: University of Chicago Press, 1987.

Hurston, Zora Neale. *Their Eyes Were Watching God*. 1937. New York: Harper & Row, Publishers, 1990.

Jones, Gayl. *Corregidora*. Boston: Beacon Press, 1975.

"Lynching: Southern Chivalry," Editorial. *The Crisis*. Mar. 1915: 225-229.

Morrison, Toni. "Home," *The House That Race Built: Black Americans, U. S. Terrain*. Edited by Wahneema Lubiano. New York: Pantheon, 1997.

Roe, Jae H. "Keeping an 'Old Wound' Alive: *The Marrow of Tradition* and the Legacy of Wilmington," *African American Review* 33.2(1999): 231-243. *JStor*. Hampton University, William R. and Norma B. Harvey Library. 10 November 2005. <http://www.jstor.org/search/>

Rudolph, Frederick. *The American University: A History*. New York: Vintage, 1962.

Sundquist, Eric. *To Wake the Nations: Race and the Making of American*. Cambridge, Harvard University Press, 1993.

Thelin, John. *A History of American Higher Education*. Baltimore: Johns Hopkins University Press, 2004.

[1] Adélékè Adéèkó, "Oral Poetry and Hegemony: Yoruba Oriki" *Dialectical Anthropology* 26: 181-192, 2001. University of Virginia. Springer Link. 23 October 2008. 190.

[2] Because *oriki* are performed within family groupings a measure of resistance is inherent in the form in so far as families challenge the social standing of others. The aggrandizement of one may come at the expense of another. Nevertheless, the performances do not challenge power set in place apart from the critique and braggadocio that might be embedded within them. Counter narratives, like those found in a bride's lament in her *oriki rare*, offer feeble resistance to larger, more compelling forces.

[3] *Oriki* are often used to praise specific individuals for personal characteristics that distinguish them as outstanding members of the society. These personal *oriki* can be numerous and pervasive and identify both great men (and less commonly women) who are both living and dead.

[4] Karin Barber. *I Could Speak Until Tomorrow: Oriki, Women and the Past in a Yoruba Town.* Edinburgh University Press for International African Institute, 1991. 81.

5 This shift in perspective begins to offer us a vocabulary for discussing the ways that the body work, which has traditionally troubled African American women, continues to restrain them in the academy. That vocabulary includes the recurring images of grave digging, sexual exploitation, reproduction, hunger, and bones.

6 I discuss Odu's calabash in Chapter 2 in relationship to Zora Neale Hurston place in the Harlem Renaissance.

7 I want to acknowledge Kimberly D. Brown whose insightful participation in my African American Women's Literature course influenced my thinking in regards to this chapter.

8 *The American Heritage Dictionary, Second College Edition*, Houghton Mifflin, 1985.

9 United States District Court Northern District of Georgia Atlanta Division "Civil Action #12972: *United States of America v The State of Georgia; The Georgia State Board of Education*" December 17, 1969.

10 This information is documented in *Professions*

[11] The following statement on an Executive Order regarding HBCUs appears on the U. S. Department of Education Office of Civil Rights web site: "On April 28, 1989, President George Bush issued Executive Order 12677 to strengthen the capacity of HBCUs to provide quality education and to increase their participation in federally sponsored programs. It mandates the taking of positive measures, by federal agencies, to increase the participation of HBCUs, their faculty and students, in federally sponsored programs. It also encourages the private sector to assist HBCUs. The Executive Order is administered by the Department's Office of Postsecondary Education - White House Initiative on Historically Black Colleges and Universities. This office also coordinates the activities of 27 federal departments and agencies in implementing Executive Order 12677. These agencies were selected for participation in the program because they account for 98 percent of federal funds directed to our colleges and universities."

www.ingramcontent.com/pod-product-compliance
Lightning Source LLC
Chambersburg PA
CBHW050205130526
44591CB00035B/2177